BE THE MOST *EFFECT*
IN YOUR BUSINESS

BE THE MOST *EFFECTIVE* MANAGER IN YOUR BUSINESS

John Lockett

THORSONS PUBLISHING GROUP

First published 1987

© J. C. LOCKETT 1987

British Library Cataloguing in Publication Data

Lockett, John
Be the most effective manager in your
business.
1. Management
I. Title
658   HD31

ISBN 0-7225-1217-1

*Published by Thorsons Publishers Limited,
Wellingborough, Northamptonshire, NN8 2RQ, England.*

Printed in Great Britain by Woolnough Bookbinding Limited,
Irthlingborough, Northamptonshire.

3   5   7   9   10   8   6   4

Contents

1
Why You Should Read This Book

To have reached the stage of reading this chapter, you must have carried out at least three purposive activities:

- You have walked into a bookshop or read a booklist.

- You have read the title and a short summary of the contents.

- You have opened the book.

This is all encouraging stuff. It means that you have an interest in effective management and also that you enjoy reading. There should be more people like you in this world.

An author has to consider carefully the type of people who will either order or pick up and buy his book. In fact, the publisher will not let an author go into print without doing this. It is the first lesson in written communication – consider your reader and what they want to get out of the book. I think that my readers are:

- Anyone in a managerial or executive position in any business organization who wants to become more effective or to help other managers to become more effective.

In particular:

- Newly appointed managers, supervisors or executives.

- Experienced executives with a responsibility for training or coaching their own staff.

- Students of management, management trainees or young employees with aspirations to become managers.

- Personnel managers or management trainers with a responsibility for developing and training staff.

The book covers a wide range of management skills. They are grouped into three main areas:

- Managing yourself.

- Communicating with other people.

- Managing your own staff.

Chapter 3 sets out the main areas which will be dealt with in the book. These skills are called *process* skills. They are skills of management and human relations which enable managers to make the most effective use of the skills which are specific to their own job (e.g. accountancy, production and marketing etc.).

These process skills are often ignored and yet are critical factors in a manager's success. The most successful foreman in an engineering shop is not the best lathe operator but is the person who can get the most out of a group of lathe operators. Operating a lathe is a specific task skill but managing effectively is a process skill which enables those technical skills to be used to their best account. To be fully effective, a manager needs to develop both technical and process skills in balance.

This book is concerned with these process skills, often neglected for a variety of reasons:

- They are things that everyone feels they already do well.

- They have been made complicated and obscure by writers and lecturers, anxious to preserve the mysteries of their craft.

- Managers are judged on results which are related to their task skills. Process skills are a means to an end, not the end itself.

This book is aimed at managers who either need or want to develop these skills. There is the potential in the book to:

- Save hours a day by better organization.

- Improve your working relationships with your boss, your colleagues and your staff.

- Make more effective decisions.

- Communicate more clearly and effectively both orally and in writing.

- Make the people who work for you more effective.

- Reduce your levels of stress and improve the quality of your life outside work.

That's why you should read this book. It will take between four and five hours to read. A small investment for such a high return.

2
The Home for Bewildered Managers

Managers are a much maligned group of people. Pressurized by bosses, envied and misunderstood by their staff and in competition with their fellow managers for scarce resources, managers need to be a resilient breed. Changes in legislation, new technology, industrial relations problems, tighter budgets and so on, create more and more problems at work for the beleaguered manager who comes home exhausted and battered, only to find that his family claims that they never see him, the dog lies in the hall unwalked and sulking and a tribe of pygmies have camped on the lawn, though the grass is so high he hasn't noticed.

To research into the problems of management, I recently visited a Home for Bewildered Managers. The warden of the home, a genial white haired gentleman, explained to me, 'This is a home where managers can rest and think out some of their problems. We see some terrible conditions here – managers who are totally disorganized; managers who are unable to form normal human relationships with their staff; terminal indecisiveness. In fact, look over there.' We watched a sober suited executive walk along a path until he came to a fork, where the path split to go round a fountain. The path met again at the other side of the fountain. The executive took one path, stopped and walked round to the other path before taking his original route, shaking his head nervously. The warden pointed, 'You see, acute indecisiveness. Before long he won't know which shoe to put on first. He was marketing director of a major food company. Look over there, the lady taking paper off one pile and putting it on to another, she was accounts manager of a large factory. She shuffled paper for so long, now she can't do anything else.'

We walked around the grounds watching managers dressed as Napoleon giving orders to non-existent staff and hysterical supervisors trampling on models of their bosses – which my guide assured me was excellent therapy. The warden showed me into his office. We sat and drank coffee at a table in the corner. I noticed that he had no desk. Reading my thoughts, he explained that one of his first patients had come into the home actually chained to a desk. Like Jacob Marley's in *The Christmas Carol*, the man's chains had been of his own making. 'Ever since then, I've avoided a desk – they're too easy to hide behind.'

'Can these people be cured?' I asked.

'Yes, of course. But the majority of cures that have been applied before they came here have only made their condition worse.' In response to my puzzled look he went on to explain, 'Well, all managers have problems of some kind. These are revealed at appraisals or interviews and then they are sent on courses. These courses are run by consultants and trainers who, not wanting to make their subject appear too straightforward, apply a series of systems, techniques and approaches which make the manager even more confused. Two years later, another fad sweeps the nation and then everyone is retrained. Finally the poor bloody manager loses touch with his normal instincts and starts to mess everything up before he finally breaks down.

'Take the management of people. The manager is a human being who gets on with other human beings at the golf club, the pub, the church or the school. He becomes a manager, goes on a human relations course and then comes back as either Napoleon or Gandhi. All through his life he makes decisions, getting some right and some wrong. He goes on a decision-making course, comes back with algorithms, decision-trees, rational processes and so on. From then on, he will not only make the wrong decisions, he will take longer to make them.

'The point is . . . management is simple but it's certainly not easy. The simple concepts of management are difficult enough to put into practice without making them more complex. What these people need is a guide to make their work more simple. That is my prescription, why don't you write it?'

I took the warden's advice. I share his belief that there are a few straightforward principles which make the whole process of management more simple. As he said, it is simple but certainly never easy.

3
Where to Find Things in the Book

The book can be read in one sitting or it can be dipped into or used as a reference book to solve particular problems. Before I left the Home for Bewildered Managers, I asked the warden for a list of symptoms which were most common to the inmates of the home. I have tried to prescribe a cure for each symptom and to direct the sufferer to a particular chapter.

Symptom	Cure	Reference
1 Rushing about in circles (known as Managers' St Vitus dance).	• Improve your organization. • Make decisions more carefully. • Delegate more effectively.	Chapter 6 Chapter 7 Chapter 22
2 Time spent on inessentials.	• Plan your time. • Clarify your objectives. • Delegate more effectively.	Chapter 6 Chapter 5 Chapter 22
3 Ineffective decisions.	• Make decisions more carefully. • Communicate decisions clearly. • Delegate unimportant decisions.	Chapter 7 Chapter 12 Chapter 22

4	Decisions not carried out by staff.	• Consult staff before making decisions.	Chapter 7
		• Communicate the decision with enthusiasm.	Chapters 7 and 12
		• Show them where they fit in.	Chapter 25

5	Problem-solving creates greater problems.	• Solve problems systematically.	Chapter 8
		• Anticipate problems.	Chapter 8
		• Manage crises, don't be controlled by them.	Chapter 20

| 6 | Difficulty in putting your case over. | • Improve your presentation skills, both written and oral. | Chapters 14 and 18 |
| | | • Communicate to both boss and staff as equals. | Chapter 13 |

7	Long and ineffective meetings.	• Clarify the purpose of the meeting.	Chapter 17
		• Provide a clear agenda.	
		• Control the meeting.	

8	Disciplinary interviews are never concluded successfully.	• Treat people as adults.	Chapter 13
		• Prepare thoroughly.	Chapter 16
		• Follow up the interview thoroughly.	Chapter 16

| 9 | Unions, suppliers and colleagues always seem to get one over on you. | • Be more assertive. | Chapter 13 |
| | | • Learn to negotiate. | Chapter 19 |

10	Your staff always make mistakes.	• Train them.	Chapter 15
		• Motivate them to work conscientiously.	Chapter 21
		• Delegate properly.	Chapter 22

| 11 | You have no one who can take over your job. | • Delegate more. | Chapter 22 |
| | | • Develop successors by coaching. | Chapter 22 |

12	Your team never quite get it together.	• Select the right people.	Chapters 16 and 24
		• Work on your leadership.	Chapter 25
		• Increase performance by motivation.	Chapter 21

| 13 | Your staff have difficulty in accepting changes. | • Communicate changes in advance. | Chapter 12 |
| | | • Manage change, don't just let it happen. | Chapter 26 |

| 14 | You never have any ideas for improving your tasks. | • Learn to think laterally. | Chapter 9 |
| | | • Give yourself time to think. | Chapter 6 |

15	You find dealing with people a strain.	• Be more assertive. • Plan your meetings. • Prepare for interviews.	Chapter 13 Chapter 17 Chapter 16
16	You find it difficult to assert yourself.	• Treat people as equals. • Improve your presentation skills. • Work at your leadership.	Chapter 13 Chapter 14 Chapter 25
17	You dread writing memos or reports.	• Learn to plan them systematically.	Chapter 18
18	You find it difficult to teach people new tasks.	• Learn basic instructional techniques. • Coach your staff rather than lecture.	Chapter 15 Chapter 22
19	You suffer from nervous tension.	• Learn to relax. • Improve your use of time.	Chapter 10 Chapter 6
20	Your career has no coherent direction.	• Set yourself objectives. • Think about your own development.	Chapters 5 and 6 Chapter 11

4
Effective Managers:
How to Recognize Them

One of the most effective ways to become an effective manager is to find one for yourself, observe its behaviour and imitate it. Unfortunately there are not too many around and so you may need some guidance to help you find one.

Habitat

The effective manager is found on the shop-floor, in the store, on the construction site or in the general office. It should be visible in the workplace not chained to a desk in its own nest or office. The effective manager may spend a little time in its office thinking but not immersed in paper or writing endless memos. The effective manager is available to its staff but not obtrusive, allowing them to get on with their own job.

Appearance

The effective manager is enthusiastic and optimistic. It has two ears and one mouth as it normally listens twice as often as it talks. It has strong feet to enable it to 'manage by walking about'. It has good co-ordination and should be able to juggle with a number of balls in the air at once.

Attitude

The effective manager is a systematic creature. Setting clear aims and planning tasks enables the effective manager to avoid the more frenetic purposeless activity which is indulged in by other members of the manager species. The effective manager is calm and controlled despite being energetic and enthusiastic.

The effective manager spends a lot of time in communication with other managers which it prefers to do face-to-face, although it gives information in writing when necessary to clarify a situation.

An interesting sideline in the behaviour of the effective manager is the behaviour of its staff. Our research and observations show that its staff always produce the best results even if they have previously worked for an ineffective manager and been regarded as poor workers.

The effective manager treats people like adults and, in turn, expects to be treated like an adult. It believes that people have a right to be treated politely and expects to be treated politely by people. It is normally neither aggressive nor submissive but can be vicious in defending its staff against attack. It is, however, firm and unrelenting in pursuit of high standards and hard on members of its staff who are not similarly interested.

Breeding

Although the effective manager is a rare breed, it will continue to survive because of its breeding habits. People who work for effective managers, themselves often become effective. In this, the effective manager is not unlike the werewolf; in all other respects this comparison does not apply. However, President Lincoln once dismissed criticism of Ulysses Grant, a general and an effective manager, by saying, 'Mad is he? Then I wish he would bite my other generals.'

Behaviour

Unlike their staff, it is often difficult to recognize what an effective manager is doing. The typist is typing so we can see what is being done; it is equally obvious what a plumber is doing when repairing a leaky cistern.

The effective manager is talking, writing or just walking about – but what is it actually doing?

If it is an effective manager it should be:

- Setting, communicating and maintaining clear and relevant aims.

- Making decisions, clarifying them and monitoring their effectiveness.

- Procuring, controlling and developing resources of manpower, money and machinery.

- Anticipating and solving problems.

- Maintaining high standards of work.

- Anticipating and managing change.

In short, the effective manager is there to make sure that the staff are working to clear guidelines and that they have the resources, training and support to do that work.

5
Setting Aims – The Crucial Stage

Would Robin Hood have been a Great British Hero if he hadn't taken aim before firing? Of course not. Do you set out on a journey without knowing where you are heading for or what you are going to do when you get there? Of course not. And yet thousands of managers every day carry out tasks with no apparent purpose and no clear end result in view. What is even worse, managers are asking their staff to carry out tasks with no clear purpose, no clear end result and no way of knowing whether or not they have been successful.

The beginning of any task should be the clear setting of aims. Why?

- Clear aims set the boundaries of a task and concentrate the mind and the activity of the person carrying it out.

- Without clear aims, the task may well end up as a completely different exercise from the one which was intended.

- People can't be motivated to carry out a project if they are unsure of what is expected of them, why they are doing it and how they will be told if they have been successful.

If Robin Hood had not aimed at a target, he would have fired in the air at random and probably hit something. Without an aim, managers will still achieve something but it will be the wrong target and the art of effective management is doing the right thing. How much better to concentrate resources on a clear and unambiguous target than to dissipate them in a vague and purposeless activity.

In almost every activity described in this book, the first

stage will be the clarification of the aim of the activity. This is not a complicated technique, it is a series of questions which should be asked before carrying anything out. Managers call meetings without a clear aim and then spend hours talking about very little. They arrange interviews and wait to see what comes up.

The main enemy of aim-setting is the euphemism flexibility. Now I am a great believer in flexibility; it's what Americans call a motherhood concept – it would be difficult for a reasonable person to be against it. Nevertheless I am against flexibility when it is used as an excuse for not clarifying the aims of an activity. Are any of these comments familiar?

Before a meeting
'I won't draw up an agenda, I'll keep the meeting flexible and deal with matters as they arise.'

Before a negotiation
'Let's not get too hung up on a game plan. I'd rather keep ourselves flexible to listen to what they have to say and respond to that.'

Before an appraisal interview
'I'm going to wait to see what points they raise.'

Before a presentation
'I'll start off by asking them what they want me to talk about.'

The people who made these comments could not achieve anything concrete, they did not know what they wanted in the first place. Furthermore, they were quite happy to hand over control to another party and so found themselves achieving somebody else's aims. The man or woman with a purpose will always defeat the man or woman without one.

The setting of aims only involves answering a few pertinent (and sometimes impertinent) questions:

- Why are we doing this? (In other words – what is the *purpose*?)

If everyone involved in a piece of work knows why they are doing it, the results are more likely to be coherent and productive. Call a meeting without a purpose and everyone turns up unprepared and fairly hostile; call a meeting with a clear purpose and everyone arrives tuned in and ready.

- What are the benefits of doing this?

By focusing attention on the positive benefits, the initiator of the work starts the process of influencing people not only to carry it out but also to do it with enthusiasm.

- What will the finished job look like?

Try to visualize the end product of an activity. If you are developing a new product, think out what gaps it will fill in the market, what it will cost and how it will be packaged. Try to make an abstract task into a concrete one.

- How will we know when we have been successful?

Set standards for success before an activity gets well underway. People need to know what they have to do to be successful so that they can appraise their own performance. It is a poor manager who sets success criteria after the event – 'We reduced our customer complaints by about five per cent, which seems satisfactory' is vague and tells us little. Setting clear criteria for success at the beginning helps everyone to assess the project or activity throughout.

The alternative to setting aims is to be aimless; the alternative to clarifying a purpose is to be purposeless. The effective manager is neither of these things and does nothing without knowing why it is being done. If you are giving work to your staff, explain why you want it and what you are looking for. If your boss gives you a project to work on without clear guidelines, ask him the four questions. He'll soon get the drift and start asking them for himself.

6
Time Management –
The Key to Effectiveness

How do managers spend their day? More to the point, how do you spend your day? When you come home at the end of the day can you say where the time has gone, what you have done with it and how much nearer you are to achieving the aims that you set yourself? That feeling of exhaustion which overwhelms you as you sit down to a cold dinner, prepared for you two hours ago; is it caused by an exhausting level of achievement or a high level of wasted expenditure? The fact that you are reading this book means that you are interested in effectiveness. Effectiveness means 'doing the right things' and is not necessarily related to a high level of activity. Of course, it is ideal if you are doing the right things at a high level of activity; but if you are not doing the right things then activity counts for nothing. If the use of time is to be effective it is to be aimed at achieving important things not an exercise in filling the day.

Of course, we all want to use our time effectively and this is one of the reasons for the popularity of time management courses. Time management courses and their accompanying systems and files are the modern executives' equivalent of the elixir of eternal youth, they are seen as an instant cure for a universal problem. People buy them and use them in the desperate hope that they will sort their schedules out. If the will is there to manage time effectively why can we not do it? I've gathered together a rogues' gallery of felons who criminally misuse their time.

The Workaholic

The workaholic actually believes that activity is a measure of effectiveness and would be shattered to find out that it is, in fact, a measure of ineffectiveness. A daughter of a friend asked her mother why Daddy was not only always late home but also worked for long hours in the study upstairs. Her mother explained that Daddy had so much work to do that he had to bring it home. With the naivety of childhood, the little girl asked, 'Why don't they put Daddy in the slow learners' group?'

That is the question we should be asking of our workaholics – 'Is the job too much for you?' Workaholism is a neurosis caused by ineffectiveness or poor job design. As with any neurosis, it is not only the neurotic who suffers – family, friends and colleagues are all affected by the habits of the workaholic. He or she knows that if the work isn't done today there are always the twilight hours to work away at the paperwork. So, of course, they can avoid doing the work at work-time and their more sensible colleagues suffer from their inadequacy.

Unfortunately, the workaholic still attracts sympathy and feels himself to be an object of admiration. Staggering home late in the evening, carrying a bulging briefcase and then rushing in early in the morning, the workaholic should be pitied and despised as an obstruction to effective management.

If you are one – stop indulging yourself. The workaholic is the most self-indulgent of this rogues' gallery. While you are enjoying your martyrdom stop and think about others – the wife or husband you never see; the children whose names you have forgotten (how on earth did you find the time to conceive them?); the subordinates whom you keep late at work and your colleagues whom you frustrate by your ineffective working methods.

If you work for one – insist firmly on your rights to a life outside work. If one works for you, do not congratulate him or her on their level of commitment and their conscientiousness – rather, chase them for not being able to do the job in the hours allotted. Show them how they can work more effectively and make sure that you've not turned them into a workaholic by creating a job that is too big for them to do.

The Procrastinator

Your grandmother told you that procrastination was 'the thief of time' and she was right. It literally means putting things off until tomorrow and the procrastinator really believes that by doing so they will either disappear or be ameliorated by the action of some fairy godmother who will appear as if in a pantomime and make everything better. In real life it doesn't happen and the longer matters are delayed, the more complex they become and thus the more difficult they are to solve. This creates the procrastinator's Catch 22, 'I procrastinate because the problem is difficult; by procrastination I make the problem more difficult.'

Procrastination is a force which puts a brake on to achievement. Procrastinators need to analyse the reason for their condition – indecision, apprehension, perfectionism, boredom and a need to work close up to deadlines are all possible reasons. Once the procrastinator understands the cause of the procrastination it becomes easier to solve. For example, I may put off carrying out a disciplinary interview with an employee because I know there will be a scene. If I face this apprehension, consider carefully how I would handle a row and prepare my interview carefully I have no longer any reason to put it off. If I continue to put it off, the problem will get worse and I will face an even bigger scene.

A major cause of procrastination is to put off large projects because of their size. This can only be resolved by breaking them up into a series of small tasks and tackling them in sequence. At the other end of the scale, small jobs are delayed because of their size. Many a great ship sank because there was a hole so small that repairing it could always wait until tomorrow. Put your small jobs into groups and give time for them in your schedule.

The Gadfly

Flitting from job to job, the gadfly spends half-an-hour on this and then flies off to do something else which seems more interesting. The gadfly never spends enough time on anything and really important jobs need concentrated periods of time. If you break an important task into two, a proportion of the second half will be spent on catching up on your thoughts in the first half. If you are a gadfly, force yourself to concentrate. Work with a clear desk so that nothing can catch your eye; screen yourself from those interesting interruptions which promise a new job to flit to; give yourself incentives to stick at a job for a sensible period of time but above all – *concentrate*.

The Yes Man

Do you find it difficult to say 'No!'? If so, you are likely to be a Yes Man (or Woman!). Subordinates, bosses, companies and colleagues are all prepared to work a willing horse. The person who says 'Yes, I'll do it' does so without thinking and probably out of a need to be loved. They aren't loved, of course; they are used and pitied but they will be encouraged by others with effusive thanks.

The 'Yes Man' has a number of corrective actions to take:

- Read chapter 13 of this book and learn to say 'No' without feeling guilty.

- Think before taking on a job:
  — Will it further your objectives?
  — Are you the right person to do the job?
  — Why are they asking you?

The Reactor

A close cousin of the Yes Man, the reactor never initiates work, but reacts to whatever pressures are put on. Every telephone call is answered and dealt with as soon as it happens, the mail has to be gone through immediately and the reactor spends the whole day achieving other people's aims and never makes time for his own. Some people are emotionally suited to this role. They like to be busy but don't like to make a decision on what needs to be done. Others fulfil the role but find it demanding and stressful. These are known as fast breeder reactors because they go off like a bomb under pressure.

A clear example of reactor behaviour can be observed on the squash court. The reactor can be seen red-faced, perspiring and out of control, reacting to the opponent's shots and never taking the initiative. The effective squash player is calmer, more controlled and always takes the initiative, playing each stroke as part of a strategy and not just hitting it desperately at the back wall.

The reactor manager is like the red-faced squash player,

batting memos and telephone calls back to the initiator, always rushing about dealing with the crises which arise as a result of never standing still long enough to anticipate them.

The Socializer

In every gathering at coffee machine, photocopier or car park, the socializer can be seen not working and actively obstructing everyone else. The socializer often justifies the condition as a means of 'oiling the wheels of human interaction' or 'taking an interest in people' or 'getting the background to where the company's at', and there is no doubt that work has a social element which cannot be ignored. A curt 'Morning' to your colleagues at the beginning of the day would not help your relationship with them but an excess of socializing destroys time, especially at the beginning of the day when people are at their freshest.

If you are a socializer, plot the time that you devote to socializing and work out how much time it takes up. Learn to be pleasant without taking up half-an-hour of everyone's time. Try to give the edited highlights of the weekend's golf rather than a stroke by stroke account of each of the thirty-six holes you played.

If you work with a socializer, visit them in their own office, so that you control your exit time. It is easier to leave a colleague's office than to evict them from yours. If they sneak into your office, then use the slightest excuse to evict them politely. The telephone ringing is an ideal opportunity to say, 'Sorry, this call could be a long one, was there anything else?'

The Nitpicker

The nitpicker is either excessively detail conscious or unable to delegate detail. Whatever the cause of the condition, the nitpicker is so concerned with the fine planning that the broad aims of the task are not considered. The nitpicker is a close relation of the perfectionist procrastinator, who holds back work until it is absolutely perfect. The nitpicker needs to learn to delegate and do a manager's job, which involves lifting the head above the detail to look at the aims and the strategy.

The Dead Bat

Every cricket fan knows that a stroke played with a dead bat has no follow through and lack of follow through is a deadly sin in the managerial black book. Many managers prepare for a meeting or interview, carry it out and then take no further steps to follow up any actions which arise from it. Any event, be it presentation, meeting or interview should not be regarded as completed until every action has been followed through. A simple bring forward system should ensure that these things are done at the right time.

Getting the Right Things Done

We have already defined effectiveness as 'getting the right things done' and this phrase is the essence of all the work carried out on time management. It includes:

- Setting priorities
- Setting clear personal aims
- Planning to achieve personal aims
- Learning to control time
- Recording and reviewing the use of time
- Finding time to think.

The important message about time management is: *If you don't control your time it will control you.*

For a manager to be effective and to achieve the important things in the job, it is vital to have control over time, to find time to do the things for which you are paid as a manager.

Reacting to crises and obeying orders have become so much part of a manager's life that many managers have forgotten how to control their time and have stopped thinking about what they want to achieve in their job – they think that someone else will help them with their problems. Some of our best management brains have become errand boys or firefighters, either carrying out orders from on high or rushing around fighting bush fires.

How do we get the right things done? Follow this seven step plan and you will take back control of your time.

Step 1 — Review your job
Every manager's job is unique. You may share a job title with other people in your company but your responsibilities will be

specific to you. Ask yourself what that job is in terms of performance. If you have a job description, that will help you but it will only take you so far. [Job descriptions are quasi-legal documents written in a bureaucratic style intended to reconcile conflicts of interests within organizations – they are only a partial guide to what you should actually be doing, they deal more specifically with the limits to your authority.]

Ask yourself (and others if you feel confident enough) what you are expected to achieve in your job. What does your boss expect? Your subordinates and your colleagues? Take a walk round your job and view it from other people's perspectives.

If you feel super-confident ask yourself, 'What would not be done around here if I fell off a cliff never to return?' If it is a very small list, you have some thinking to do.

Step 2 — Give yourself an appraisal

Ask yourself what are your strengths and weaknesses. What are the things you do well and what areas of specialized knowledge do you bring to your job? Are you making the most of these and can you use them more effectively to achieve higher quality results?

What are your weaknesses? The things you don't do too well or knowledge that you need to acquire to become more effective in your work? Do *you* need to improve in these areas or are they being covered by someone else in your team?

Improvements will not come automatically. They need to be thought out, planned and reviewed regularly. Only consider skills and knowledge that are relevant to your job.

Step 3 — Look around you

Priorities change with the environment you work in. Look around at your business, your factory or office. What needs changing? What systems don't work? Which people need careful monitoring?

Look ahead. What new technology may be introduced? What are your competitors doing? How will your customers' needs change? Is there legislation in the pipeline which will affect the way you do your job? Anticipate changes and plan to assimilate them; if you wait until they arrive then you will leave yourself no option but to react to them.

The expert surfer sees waves beginning and rides them to a successful conclusion; the beginner only sees the waves when they are too big to get on to and is swept away by them.

Step 4 — Set yourself clear aims

Thinking about your job, your skills and the environment that you work in should lead you to think about some of the areas that you want to attend to. In the past you have probably thought 'I ought to do something about that' in the same way as every New Year's Day you resolve to stop smoking and be nicer to the in-laws.

If we are to make these into more than vague resolutions, then we should first make them into an aim with a purpose, clear ideas about what we are trying to achieve and a sensible way of measuring our success.

Step 5 — Write out a plan

Setting an aim is only the first stage. The next is to translate the aim into a plan. Writing down a plan makes a stronger commitment and it also protects the fallible memory. Answer the questions:

When can it be done by? or
When does it need to be ready?
Who will help me carry it out?
Whose agreement do I need?
Where and *how* will I carry it out?

Set a deadline for the plan and include interim checkpoints. The deadline should be stretching, neither impossibly hard nor ridiculously easy.

Step 6 — Control your diary

Leave regular times in your diary to work on these important tasks, otherwise the work will all be done the day before the deadline; hardly a recipe for high quality work. Protect these chunks of thinking time by whatever devious means you can. Work for a couple of hours at home; sit in a motorway service station (I am writing this paragraph in a Little Chef on the M4); lock yourself in the toilet or any other appropriate place. If you can't prevent an intrusion into this thinking time, then re-make an appointment with your brain and write another chunk of thinking time into your diary.

Step 7 — Review

Review the progress towards achieving your aims regularly. Are there any changes in priority? Have some changes become more important? Do you need to speed up work in some areas? Don't be afraid to review your aims in the light of changing circumstances, provided that you replace them with other specific aims and don't just fall into aimlessness. Every now and then devote some of your thinking time to a total review of priorities and encourage your staff to do the same. All of this demands personal organization to control the small reactive tasks. The better organized you can be in handling the small tasks, the more time you can use to work on the important projects. Luckily there are a number of factors which can help you in your struggle.

Your secretary

If you have the luxury of a secretary or PA you have a tremendous advantage, provided that the two of you are a team. In my experience, secretaries have a much greater flair for personal organization than most managers and the effective manager harnesses this flair to the benefit of both parties. Like a good tennis doubles partnership, the boss/secretary relationship hinges on tacit understanding based on clear communication and preparation.

To paraphrase an army maxim, 'There are no bad secretaries, only bad bosses'. Treat your secretary as a robot typist and taker of shorthand and that's what you will get; treat her (or him!) as the essential part of your team and you will increase your effectiveness significantly.

Never underestimate a secretary's job. They should be reading this book because it is a management role demanding organization, the assertive handling of senior people, communication skills and the ability to influence their boss (yes, you!). If you are looking for a present for your secretary, you should look no further than this book. It would help your secretary to do the job more effectively as well as explaining what you are up to.

- Discuss your work with your secretary so s/he knows what you are doing.

- Agree with your secretary how your work should be organized and review it together regularly.

- Delegate work carefully and then don't hover.

- Consider your secretary's schedule as important and don't treat it as something which is just intended to fit round yours.

- If you can't always be polite, at least give your secretary adequate gale warnings when your Beaufort Scale is going over Force 10.

The tools of your trade which you and your secretary (or you on your own if you don't have a secretary) should be using are set out below. Like any tool, correct and effective use makes them an aid to good organization; using them the wrong way makes them a barrier.

Diary
Use your diary as a planner and a to-do list, not just as an appointments book. Some of the time systems on the market can help you to do this. Make sure that your secretary knows what is in your diary.

Control your diary, don't allow it to clog up for weeks in advance with trivia so that you can't fit in the important things when you need to. If people want to take up your time, agree a purpose and a time limit. Salesmen, for example, will take up your whole day unless you give a clear time limit and it is more helpful for both of you to do that before the appointment rather than saying in the middle, 'I've another appointment in ten minutes, could you speed it up?'

Desk
Don't use your desk top as a large flat pending tray. A stacked desk may make you look busy but it is a distraction from the task that you are working on. Sadly, an empty desk is seen by many not as a sign of efficiency but of lethargy. 'You have a tidy desk so you obviously aren't busy' is a particularly irritating put-down to the effective manager.

Use a hanging file system for current projects and IN, OUT and PENDING trays for moving paper across. Agree a system for weeding out paper with your secretary and encourage her to take the initiative in emptying the OUT tray regularly.

Filing cabinet
Filing cabinets should be filled sparingly and emptied regularly. Keep one copy only of retained paperwork and weed out irrelevant letters as regularly as possible. Agree some guidelines for reviewing files with your secretary and ignore the people who say that they always need a piece of paper the day after they have thrown it away. These old management sayings have no basis in reality.

Waste paper baskets
'File under WPB' is the cry of the effective manager. If you don't need it – ditch it!

Briefcase
A briefcase is not just something to carry two egg sandwiches and a newspaper. If you need to travel regularly, organize your briefcase like a mobile office. Always have pens, notebooks and any telephone lists you need with you and carry your diary/planner and any business reading in your briefcase. Two hours on a train, in a 'plane or in an airport lounge can be a week's thinking time. With the right equipment in your briefcase you have the information to make that thinking time extremely effective.

If there is a summary of the skills of time management it is this – decide what are the most important things to do and make time to do them. Simple, yes, but not easy.

Self Development Activities

1.   Design a simple time log and then for one day record accurately how you spend your time. Mark down interruptions especially. Then review the data and analyse:

- How much time did you spend actually working?

- How much time did you spend working on important work rather than reactive tasks?

- What interrupted you and how can that be prevented?

- How can you improve your use of time?

Carry this exercise out every three months or so.

7
Making Effective Decisions

Inspired by TV soap operas and monetarism, the macho manager is walking tall across the commercial prairies. Modelled on J.R. Ewing and Alexis Carrington (yes, women managers can be more macho than the male) with antecedents going back to Tamburlaine the Great and Ivan the Terrible, they are tough and cruel, always ready for a showdown and totally unloved by their staff and the colleagues whom they have ridden over in their Ford Granadas to get to the top. Pardon the excessive use of cliché but the macho manager is a cliche, a manager desperate to preserve a persona, which is always 'non grata'. Part of that persona is the misused word – decisive.

The real macho manager would not be reading this book. Firstly, Real Men Don't Read Books. Reading is for wimps, macho managers spend their time drinking or playing macho games like Russian roulette. Secondly, the macho manager doesn't want to be effective, merely to appear effective and, thirdly, the macho manager can't always read.

If we asked the macho manager to describe how to make a decision, how to be *decisive* he would make the following points:

- Decisions are to be made alone. Other people have nothing to contribute to your decision so don't ask them.

- Never consider alternatives, they only confuse the issue. Do things the way they have always been done or take the first course of action which presents itself.

- Make decisions quickly. A snappy decision is always better than one that has been thought out. Thinking only dilutes gut feelings.

- Communicate decisions by memo, giving clear orders. Employees like people who know what they want. It gives them confidence.

- Don't waste time monitoring decisions. If you explain things clearly, people will carry them out promptly.

Sadly, the macho managers have convinced some of their colleagues that some, if not all, of these factors are correct. In reality, decision-making is a process of gathering information, considering aims, generating alternatives, trying to influence people to carry out the decision with enthusiasm and checking to see that it has been carried out. Decisiveness is a quality of making effective decisions, not fast ones.

Gathering Information

This stage is two-fold: information about the boundaries of the decision and information about the content of the decision.

- Make sure that you have clarified that the decision is yours to take and that you are sure of the boundaries of the decision. The boundaries of the decision are matters like timing, resources available, who needs to authorize the decision and so on. Ask yourself 'What is my boss expecting from this decision?' or if you are the initiator 'What is the purpose of this decision?'

- Ensure that your decision is based on facts. Work hard to ensure that your information is accurate and measurable. Decision making is a systematic process which needs to be underpinned by facts.

- Consult people who are going to be affected by your decision. They have information, opinions and perspectives which can be of great use to you in making your decision. You need that information if your decision is to be effective. What is probably more important is that if you fail to consult people before you make a decision, you will find it doubly hard to motivate them to carry the decision out afterwards. People will not always volunteer information, they need to be asked. Consultation is not a form of weakness, it is an important step in making a good decision.

Clarifying Your Aims

You have already asked yourself or your boss the purpose of the decision. You now need to clarify the aim further. Try to visualize what the successful end product of your decision would look like and write down all the factors which will have an effect on it.

For example, when you want to buy a house you consider a number of factors: price range, location, size, type of heating, garden, garage, etc.

You can then build up a description of the type of house you are looking for. This then gives you a framework of factors which enables you to review sensibly the flood of brochures which come from the estate agent. Without this framework, the whole process would be chaotic and you would be rushing from ten-bedroom mansion to one-bedroom maisonette in a search for something elusive that you would recognize as soon as you saw it.

Clarifying aims does two things:

- It concentrates the mind of the decision-maker on the needs which the decision is supposed to fulfil.

- It prevents the decision-maker from considering every possible alternative in detail and enables him to give more attention to the alternatives which are more likely to meet those needs.

Try to break those factors up into two types – those which are essential and those which are merely desirable. For your final decision to be effective, it must meet all your basic requirements and as many of the desirables as possible. For example, you may want to recruit an engineer to work in a petrochemical plant in Saudi Arabia. It may be essential that the successful candidate has a degree in engineering and experience in the petrochemical industry; thus in your preselection you would only pick candidates with these two qualifications. It may be desirable that the candidate is under thirty and has experience of working in Saudi Arabia as well as a number of other qualities. You would like to appoint someone with as many of these qualities as possible but the absence of one or more of them would not debar a good candidate.

Considering Alternative Solutions

The effective decision-maker tries to develop a number of alternatives, but not too many. Taking the first, the easiest or the traditional option will take up little time but the decision-maker, and their boss, will probably be disappointed in the final quality of the result. By reducing the number of options to one or two, the decision-maker curtails that thinking time which is necessary to create a high quality decision. The decision may be barely satisfactory but why settle for satisfaction when you can achieve excellence?

How many of us when recruiting staff would only interview one person and then take them on because they appeared to be 'in spec'? We always want a choice of candidates so that we not only meet our basic requirements but also recruit the best person available.

It is also possible to consider too many options and this is why we need to work hard at clarifying our aims at the very beginning. When we advertise a job vacancy we do not interview everyone; we interview those who meet our basic requirements so that we are not wasting valuable time on people who are unlikely to meet our job specification.

Making the Decision

This is the crunch time. You have, on the one hand, a set of clear criteria and, on the other, a range of alternative solutions. Like a magician, you should now be able to put both sets into a box, say a few appropriate words and wait for the decision to pop up like early morning toast. It is not as easy as that, but it is almost as simple! Follow the sequence in this recipe.

Recipe for an Effective Decision

Ingredients:

One or two sheets of paper
A pen or pencil
A set of factors which the decision needs to fulfil
A number of alternative solutions
Some thinking time
A large whisky (optional)

Method:
1   Take the sheet of paper and place it in front of you in landscape format.
2   List the decision factors along the left hand side of the page, placing the essential ones at the top.
3   Draw a line under the essential factors.
4   Write the alternative solutions along the top of the page, drawing them up in columns.
5   Take the first factor and check whether each alternative meets it. If it does, reward it with a tick; it not, with a cross.
6   Do this for each factor above the line.
7   Before moving below the line, discard any alternative which attracted a cross. Any alternative which fails to meet your basic requirements does not deserve any further consideration.
8   Then go below the line. Make sure that your other factors are in order of importance.
9   Take the highest priority factor and assess how each alternative meets it. Give two ticks for any alternative which meets it clearly, one tick for any alternative which narrowly meets it and no ticks for alternatives which don't meet it.

You now have a picture of how the alternative solutions meet the requirements of the decision. Any alternative which has not met the basic requirements has been discarded, allowing you to focus attention on those which meet those requirements.

10   Select two or three alternatives which appear to meet your remaining high priority factors better than the others.
11   Examine both the positive and negative aspects of selecting those alternatives.
12   Select the alternative which meets the most high priority decision factors and poses the fewest problems. This is in the final stages a question of judgement. It is, however, a judgement which you have been able to exercise without wasting your energy on the whole range of options.

From Decision to Action

Now you have conceived and given birth to a bonny bouncing decision. All that you have to do now is to get it to adulthood as a mature, active piece of management thinking. How do you do that?

- *Get the necessary agreement.* If you need someone else's authority to put your decision into effect then get it. Present your decision to them in the form that you have carried it out. This is where a systematic approach is so much clearer to present than a mumbled, 'It seemed like a good idea at the time'. Your boss will ask 'What were you trying to achieve?' and 'What alternatives did you consider?' and 'What made you decide on X?' You will have the answer to all these questions if you have worked logically.

- *Communicate to the people who ought to know.* Get the people together and brief them in a group, giving them time to ask questions and clarify details. Communicate as if you believe in the decision and deliver your briefing in a way that will inspire and motivate people to carry it out. Back up your briefing with a written summary, so that even if your team disperse to the five continents, they will have something to refer to. It is up to you to ensure that the details are clear; in a state of confusion, people will often do what they think is right rather than check with the originator of the decision.

- *Communicate to the people who might like to know.* Don't restrict your briefing to the 'need to knows' unless the matter is so confidential that a limited circulation is necessary. Your decision may be relevant to other people in the organization, who may be working in some area which is complementary to yours or who have information which may enhance your decision. You may not have consulted them before you made it, but let them know what's going on when the decision has been made.

- *Check that your decision is being carried out.* Your decision may be fully grown and in action but it still needs a little gentle chaperoning. Don't leave it to its own devices but check that it is doing what you intended it to do. Monitoring a decision is the area that is most often forgotten. The decision is made and communicated, so we feel relieved that it is all over and turn to the next decision without checking that the first decision has been carried out. Here lies the path to crisis management. A decision unmonitored can be reproducing problems like bacteria in a drain before reproducing a plague of crises which erupt everywhere.

The effective manager considers the likely problems and watches carefully for them. Sitting in your office waiting for someone to ring up with problems is no way to find them. The people out there may not recognize them as problems until it's too late; if you are monitoring carefully you should be able to anticipate problems and solve them early before they develop into a crisis.

- *Check that your decision is still appropriate.* Don't assume that a decision once made will always be effective. Review your decisions to make sure that they are still the most appropriate way of doing things. If they are no longer relevant start again by clarifying the aims and reviewing the alternative solutions.

When all this is not Appropriate

- *Routine decisions.* Don't carry out this procedure laboriously for every small decision – (Do I tick box A or B?). Occasionally review your daily routine decisions – can they become automatic or do they need making at all?

- *Emergency decisions.* When you hear the fire alarm ring, don't gather people together and say 'Now, what are we trying to achieve here?' Just get the hell out by the quickest way!

Try to anticipate emergencies and develop drills to help overcome them. The army's performance in battle is only as good as the techniques practised to perfection in peacetime. The middle of a battle is no place to say 'I wonder if we could try this manoeuvre a different way?'

Self Development Activities

1 Read the newspapers for examples of government decisions, review their effectiveness in the light of their aims, generation of alternatives and method of communication.

2 Look back on your own decisions. How could they have been made more effective?

3 What are your strengths and weaknesses when making decisions? Do you suffer from a lack of consultation, absence of alternatives, unenthusiastic communication or lack of follow-through? How can you eliminate your weaknesses?

8
Problems – Their Prevention and Cure

Does this type of quote seem familiar to you?

'The clever so-and-so who said that "there were no problems, only opportunities" should have worked here for a week. He'd have soon changed his tune.'

'Let's face it, Adrian. People are a problem.'

'Endeavour to Mission Control, Houston. We have a problem.'

'That's a Y.P. – Your Problem.'

Part of a manager's job is to solve problems. If there were no problems, there would be no need for managers. Most problems are caused by people because most systems are run by people and problems can only be solved by people. We blame computers for sending gas bills for £10 million to old age pensioners but we know that it is the programmer or operator who is to blame.

Problems come in various sizes and complexities. They are often a bouillabaisse of rumours, half-truths, intuition and fact. The manager has to extract the meat from this fishy stew and try to analyse it. Although dealing with problems is a major part of the manager's job, very few managers have been trained in analysing and solving problems. As a result, five types of behaviour prevail.

The headless chicken
This is characterized by a flurry of brainless activity. When a problem occurs, the headless chicken meets it by rushing about in a fruitless search for a solution. Before he drops exhausted to the floor, the headless chicken may actually create more problems and will certainly not solve the difficulty in question. Why? Because the poor decapitated fowl has no brain and no eyes and the two skills in problem

solving are thinking logically and observing carefully. The most unhelpful reaction when a problem occurs is panic. When managers panic they lose their objectivity and instead of analysing the problem, they create even more.

The overkiller

A close relation of the macho manager, the overkiller believes that the intellectual exercise of trying to establish the cause of the problem is strictly for the wimps. The overkiller takes swift and immediate action even if it is costly and irreparable. Typically overkill cures kill the patient before the problem does.

An employee with twenty years service starts to become less reliable? Don't muck around with finding out what the problem is, sack him! Problems with quality control? Don't sit about trying to work it out, close the plant. Your wife has a slight cough? Don't send her to the doctors, divorce her or shoot her.

The overkiller forgets that the aim of problem solving is to solve the problem with a minimum of disruption and cost.

The dyspeptic

So called because he works on 'gut reaction', the dyspeptic knows everything that can go wrong on the plant or in the store and so his immediate reaction to a problem is to take some drastic action based on a similar problem in the past. Because he is sometimes right in his diagnosis, he becomes, in his own mind, a mystic and because of his flair for self-publicity, a legend builds up around him. People say, 'There's a problem on number 3 autoclave; call for Harry: he fixed it in 1953.' Harry, of course, is wrong far more often than he is right but these mistakes are soon forgotten.

Instinct is no substitute for systematic thinking. Often the person with the most technical knowledge on a subject finds problem-solving very difficult. They are too close to it and make assumptions that the layman wouldn't make.

The blame-thrower

The blame-thrower doesn't want to know what caused the problem; he wants to know who. Of course, this has a tremendous impact on the search for a solution; everyone becomes so much more open and co-operative when they know that someone is looking round for a scapegoat to sacrifice!

Another blame-thrower ploy is to keep quiet throughout the problem-solving, wait until the guilty man is named and then nail him to the factory gates 'pour encourager les autres'. This seems very effective until the next time there is a problem. The previous victim is still nailed there as a reminder to the others of the folly of frankness in the presence of the blame-thrower and the search for the problem will again be hampered.

The ostrich
Quite simply, the ostrich believes that if ignored problems will go away. They won't.

The essential fact to grasp about problem solving is the question of change. A problem is the gap between expectations and reality and something must change to create the problem. Take your car; it is performing well, you enjoy driving it and no mechanical problems are apparent. Then suddenly the running is rough and the car is no longer a pleasure to drive. Either something has gone wrong with the car or the uses to which it is now put are causing the car to react. Perhaps someone else is driving it or you've taken to driving it across fields. Whatever the problem, something has changed and it is almost certain that the problem will be connected with that change.

The analysis of a problem focuses on the area of change in a systematic way. The problem-solver is like a scientist looking through a microscope; focusing relentlessly on the cause of the problem, discarding red herrings and false leads. Approach your problem like a doctor interviewing a patient, try to piece together the problem by asking the right sort of questions.

Step 1 — 'Now, what appears to be the trouble?'
Ask yourself how the problem manifests itself. At this stage, the doctor would be happy with a short description such as 'It's me throat' or 'I'm not regular'.

Step 2 — 'Where exactly does it hurt?
This step is a detailed gathering of information. Some facts the doctor will check for himself – temperature and blood-pressure. For some the doctor will rely on the description from the patient. The questioning will be specific, aimed at disqualifying certain areas of investigation. The doctor wants to find out the boundaries of the condition and the detailed

effects – Where does it hurt? (And, Where doesn't it?). When do you feel pain? (And, When don't you?). Is it a short stabbing pain or a long-drawn-out ache?

This step produces valuable information and enables the doctor (or in your case, the manager) to focus attention on the area in which the problem is located and, equally important, where it is not located.

Step 3 — 'Have you changed your diet or anything?'
The doctor tries to assess if there are any changes which may have brought about the problem. Stress at work, diet, family illness perhaps. At work, the manager must consider what has changed – a new system, a new employee, a change in machinery or supplier. Can this change be connected with the problem?

The manager must also, like the doctor, analyse the problem, comparing the areas in which the problem has occurred with those in which it hasn't and asking why.

Step 4 — 'What are the possible causes?'
The doctor and the manager should now be able to list some of the possible causes of the problem. Their analysis should enable them to see some sort of pattern emerging in the disease and at this stage they should list the factors which may have caused the problem.

Step 5 — 'Aha. I think you've got X.'
Test the possible causes against the information available and you should be able to discard any possibilities which do not match the facts. You should now be able to arrive at the most probable cause; remembering that a problem can sometimes be caused by the interaction between a number of factors, which may look like more than one cause.

Step 6 — 'Let me test this out.'
To make the most probable cause into the true cause, you have to test it. The questioning technique takes you so far but verification has to be more concrete and should be a physical test. If the verification is positive, move on to the next step. If negative, go back and check your facts and analysis.

Step 7 — 'I've prescribed this for you.'
When you understand the cause of the problem, you can then start to prescribe a solution. You are now back to the decision-making process because there is possibly more than one

solution to the problem. Your solution should be long term, i.e. it should prevent the problem from recurring. Short term palliative measures are unsatisfactory, they only lead you back to step 1 in the long term.

An Ounce of Prevention

Of course, the ideal strategy is to prevent problems arising at all. Again preventing problems is simple but not easy.

- Monitor your decisions carefully. Don't wait for problems to arise, go out and find them and snuff them out before they grow too big.

- In any project, focus your attention on the areas which are critical to success. What problems can arise there?

- After any crisis, review the cause and make sure that drills are put into place to stop the same crisis happening again.

- In any activity, write down what can go wrong. If you can't prevent it, consider what you would do if it happened.

People are a Problem

People problems are no different from any other. They can be solved using the same approach as commercial or technical problems. They are, however, often related to feelings and emotions and thus need handling very carefully. They do have a cause and once the cause is discovered, a solution can be found in the same way as any other problem.

The important thing to avoid in people problems is overkill. Many managers are like the Queen in *Alice in Wonderland* and would dearly love to execute staff for poor performance. They are limited to the cries 'Sack him' or 'Don't give me all that, just get rid of her' which every personnel manager knows are the prelude to a lengthy battle.

The other extreme is to be an ostrich. The longer people problems are left alone, the more unpleasant they become. Act quickly but sensitively and you will be well on the way to a solution.

Self Development Activities

1   Look back over past problems and consider how they were solved. Could they have been solved better?

2   Consider the five poor problem-solvers? Which category do you come into? Work out a plan to strengthen your skills in this area.

9
Creative Thinking

Which management tool possesses the following features? It weighs 3 lb, is portable, consists of 10^9 cells (10,000 of which are destroyed every day), is grey with pink lines, is grossly under-utilized, and no training is given in its use.

If you've not worked it out yet, you are not using it. Of course, it is the brain. The effective manager uses his brain to save his feet. There are two main principles behind this chapter:

- The brain is under-used. It has an almost infinite capacity and we never get even remotely near to straining it.

- Thinking is a skill and thus can be taught. It is, unfortunately, rarely taught in schools, colleges or training centres.

One important misconception to clear away is that clever people are logical and imaginative thinkers and people with lower IQs are irrational and dull. IQ tests are tests of potential and tell us very little about the quality of thinking. A recent American study showed no significant correlation between a high IQ and creativity, independence, intellectual curiosity, knowledge, fluency or activity. In terms of brainpower – 'it ain't what you got, it's the way that you use it'. This should be a consolation to all those managers who don't do well in IQ tests and a spur to those who do.

Without being too technical, the brain may be defined as being in two halves connected by a cable of nerve fibres. Each half deals with a different form of activity. The left side deals with the more scientific activities – logic, reasoning, deduction, analysis. The right side deals with the artistic activities – music, imagination, colour, art.

Most activities need both sides to function in balance at different times. Problem analysis is a left-sided activity but finding an appropriate solution can be a right-sided area. Generating alternatives for decision making is imaginative, comparing them to the original aims is logical and left-sided. Artists need a sense of symmetry and pattern as well as colour; scientists need to jump over logic barriers to make new discoveries – Einstein is alleged to have initiated his thinking on relativity by imagining a journey on a ray of sunlight; he then pursued this insight by relentless logic.

These two sides of the brain create distinct thinking styles:

Convergent – convergent thinking is always trying to narrow the focus down towards one solution. It is deductive thinking, logical and sequential. Many of the techniques in this book are convergent and it is this style of thinking which managers find the most natural.

Divergent – divergent thinking is trying to break out, to diverge from an existing pattern. The divergent thinker is not bound to logic or precedent but can take conceptual leaps to new standpoints to consider problems from a different perspective. Divergent thinking is less common in managers because many organizations discourage original thinking and so many managers get little chance to practice it.

I want to concentrate on creative thinking for the remainder of this chapter. Organizations, departments, working parties and teams grow on ideas. Without ideas, companies do the same things until they are overtaken by a changing world. Darwin taught the world that effective animals survive by adapting to their environment; that adaptation can be a new idea or a new application of an old idea. The dinosaur, the former market leader in the animal world, refused to adapt or develop. Suddenly, a change in the market place wiped the species out – an example for us all.

Creative Thinking

The creative thinker is an unpopular animal in many corporation jungles. Challenging well established conventions, wanting to do things differently, looking at things in a new way: these are all habits which are not viewed too kindly in the modern corporation where a mindless obedience to company policy coupled with a determination not to rock the organizational boat are often prime determinants of success.

There are individual barriers to creative thinking – making assumptions, stereotyping, fear of failure and pure intellectual laziness. These barriers need to be removed if companies are to develop the ideas that they need for survival.

Thinking is a process in which brain cells link together in a pattern. If the pattern is successful, it becomes established. Thoughts tend to head for that particular pattern like water, which always follows the line of least resistance. The water becomes a river; the thought becomes a habit and instead of being just one option it becomes the only option and becomes more and more deeply entrenched.

Creative thinking has to burst out of these restrictions and many of the techniques of creative thinking do just that. Some ultra-rational managers find the techniques trivial but if they are happy to remain automata then that is a matter for their own conscience.

Creative thinking can be done individually or in groups. Group thinking can add to the quantity of ideas and to the cross-fertilization of ideas but an individual, in the right frame of mind, can generate a great quantity of ideas.

There are a number of principles which underpin all creative thinking techniques:

1   The objective of creative, or lateral, thinking is to generate ideas. The breeding of ideas is inhibited by the knowledge that they will be strangled at birth by a critical boss. Evaluating ideas is a process of analytical thinking and comes into effect only after all ideas have been brought out. It is important to suspend judgement until this stage.

2   Instead of evaluating and criticizing ideas, participants in creative thinking sessions should combine and improve on the ideas that have already been suggested. They should use the positive expression 'Yes, and . . . rather than the negative 'Yes, but . . .' 'Yes, but . . .' in effect means 'No' and thus stops people putting forward new ideas.

3   The generation of ideas is a process which tries to break out of the entrenched patterns of thinking. In order to do this the creative thinker has to reduce inhibitions and undo the shackles of company policy. Wild and unconventional ideas have the effect of breaking those patterns and the process of creative thinking should be accompanied by off-beat

suggestions and humour. Once the mould of vertical thinking is broken, then the wild ideas can lead on to more useful ideas.

There are a number of techniques for stimulating ideas. Many of them are described in the Edward de Bono works on lateral thinking. The most commonly used technique is brainstorming.

Brainstorming
Brainstorming is a means of generating a large number of ideas from a group of people in a short time. In essence, it consists of asking a group of people to think of as many solutions as possible to a particular problem. This may often mean restating the problem and thinking of wild solutions instead of those which are the most common. All ideas should be written down on a flip-chart without any criticism. If a participant criticizes the idea of another, they will inhibit not only the originator of the idea but some of the more timid participants who may be afraid of their own ideas being criticized. The session must have a chairman who will set the ground rules for the brainstorming meeting at the very beginning.

Evaluation of the ideas comes later. Even this stage depends on lateral thinking, in reviewing the application of the solution to the problem. This stage also demands some vertical thinking; evaluation is a process part-critical, part analytical but part creative.

How to Improve the Creativity of Your Staff

- Don't be critical of new ideas as soon as you hear them. Encourage people to develop new ideas and talk them through with you. Never criticize imaginative thinking, save your criticism for the person who hasn't had a new idea since they joined.

- Get people together for a concentrated period of time to work out a solution to a problem or a means to exploit an opportunity. Eight people locked together for a day can generate more ideas than they would in a year of one hour committee meetings.

- If you have a team member who has myriad wild ideas of which only one in ten works, don't cramp their style. Put them with someone who can evaluate ideas logically without stemming the creative flow.

- Make sure people enjoy work. Happy people with a sense of humour give off ideas; demotivated people couldn't give a damn.

- Don't steal credit for someone else's ideas, otherwise they won't bring them to you again.

Self Development Activities

1   Look at a brick. How many uses can it be put to? Aim for 100 in fifteen minutes.

2   Think about your management style. Do you encourage ideas or are you too quick to spot the flaw? Remember, you are a manager and not a diamond sorter.

10
Managing Stress

Without stress, nothing is achieved. A healthy level of stress is necessary for us to achieve anything. The butterflies in our stomach before we make a speech are a sign of stress but without that we would not produce a high quality performance. One of the great parliamentary performers, Harold Macmillan, admitted to feeling sick for hours before a major speech. The stress mechanism is the primeval response to external threats. It enabled our Neanderthal ancestors to meet the physical challenges of their environment. In essence the 'flight or fight' mechanism is started by the hormone adrenalin pouring into the bloodstream; then the heartbeat increases, muscles tense, blood clotting time shortens (to reduce the effect of wounds), the rate of breathing increases and the body is ready for action. These responses were appropriate for dealing with a mammoth; they are still appropriate for dealing with a mugger but they are not appropriate for dealing with the tax return, a militant shop steward or an idiotic driver overtaking on the inside lane.

If we are to harness the benefits of stress and to minimize its harmful effects, we must control it rather than become its victim. There is no doubt that stress is both a major cause of death and a cause of ineffectiveness in managers. It also damages the quality of life itself. In order to control it, we must consider the causes and the symptoms before looking at ways of relieving stress.

What Causes Stress?

There are a number of areas of life which particularly cause stress. I have broken them down into six areas: work, people, time, environment, domestic and personality.

Work

The manager is not only responsible for managing his stress but for preventing excessive stress in his subordinates. The causes of stress at work are mainly paradoxical. It is a narrow path to tread as, for example, working too hard is as stressful as not having enough to do; promotion is stressful, so is being passed over for promotion; the massive responsibilities of chairmanship are as stressful as the tedium of working on an assembly line; lack of work, in terms of unemployment, is stressful so is relocation to a new job. Work is definitely bad for your health.

People

In the same way as the work-related stressors are paradoxical, so are some of the people-related stressors. Crowds cause stress, so does loneliness. Wives and husbands cause stress, so does not finding a suitable mate and, of course, so do divorce, separation and the death of a spouse. Children are massive causes of stress, but so is sterility. In the work setting, confrontation with people is stressful but so is displacing aggression to avoid conflict. Bosses cause their subordinates stress and managing people is far more stressful than managing machines.

Time

Being constantly in a hurry is stressful. In the modern business world time is at a premium, hence the current spate of time management courses. Failing to plan and anticipate problems increases the number of crises in a manager's life, crises lead to more crises and cause an increasing amount of stress. The cycle of crisis is exacerbated because decisions made in a crisis are usually not well thought out and sow the seeds for yet more crises. A tight schedule is also stressful; that feeling that grips the heart as the hour of an appointment comes up when you are sitting in a traffic jam on the North Circular Road, can only be sustained so often.

Environment

Overcrowding and noise are major irritants both at home and in the workplace. Those irritants become major causes of stress if they are unremitting. The example of high rise housing over the last twenty years shows that people can only live in crowded conditions for so long without contracting nervous or psychosomatic illness. Also we tense muscles against noise, and consequently suffer headaches and high blood-pressure.

Home life

These causes are often a mixture of people and environment. A secure and happy home life is a great reliever of stress but any disruption to that life carries over into work. Marriage brings an opportunity to share problems and experience but it can also bring about unhappiness. Workaholics, who try to spend every hour at work, can often suffer for this in terms of a bitter and resentful spouse. On the Holmes-Rahe scale (a scale which weights the problems which commonly cause stress), the highest stressors are to do with disruption of normal home life – death, divorce, imprisonment and separation. Work-related stress comes lower down the scale.

Personality

The American psychologists split mankind into two personality types – 'A' and 'B'. Type A are competitive aggressive people who drive themselves and their staff very hard. They are prone to stress and especially to heart attacks. Type Bs are calmer, more easy-going and more likely to plan ahead to avoid stress. In fact, there are few 'pure' type A or Bs and the typology is more of a scale of behaviour. Type Bs are not immune to stress but they are more likely to soak it up than As. Some Type As are stress carriers, impervious to stress themselves but likely to pass it on to others.

Some symptoms of stress

Physical
1 Stomach pains and digestive problems
2 Muscular tension
3 Palpitations
4 Diarrhoea
5 Heart disease
6 High cholesterol
7 Fatigue
8 Headaches
9 Asthma
10 Susceptibility to colds and flu

Psychological
1 Disturbed sleep
2 Sexual problems
3 Irritability
4 Dependence on drugs and alchohol
5 Inability to concentrate
6 Depression
7 Obesity or anorexia
8 Obsessions
9 Heavy smoking
10 Breathlessness

All the above, and many others, can be the symptoms of stress. They all damage the quality of life, to the extent that they can be fatal! The way to relieve these symptoms of stress is set out below.

How do you Relieve Stress?

There are a variety of ways to relieve stress. I have categorized them as follows:

Self awareness

A manager has a dual role in coping with stress – there is a need both to cope with your own problems and those of your staff. In both cases self awareness is an important first step. You need to be clear about what causes your stress and what symptoms become apparent. An awareness of the early signs of stress allows a manager to take remedial action before something serious happens. The little signs of stress are insignificant in themselves but, like the ignition light in a car, you ignore them at your peril. Likewise, if you understand what causes stress, it is then possible to take more care in particular areas of work. If time pressure is a critical problem, the effective manager reduces stress by taking more care in planning time.

Personal organization

Working in a mess, writing notes on scraps of paper, always in a hurry to get to appointments – all these are causes of stress. Plan in advance to reduce unnecessary crises. Keep a diary and a 'To Do' list and make sure that at the beginning of each day you plan the day ahead. You may not always carry out the plan to the letter but you will only achieve things if you plan to achieve them. Keep a tidy desk and attack your paperwork regularly. Paperwork, like mowing lawns, is easier to do little and often.

Stretching objectives

Boredom is a major cause of stress and yet no one needs to be bored. Consider your area of responsibility, actively seek out areas which need improvement or which may need working on in future, then set yourself goals to achieve them. This is a positive attitude to life. If you are unhappy with something then work hard to change it, if it can't be changed, endure it with patience. An old prayer reads 'Lord, let me change what can be improved; let me endure what can't be changed and give me the wisdom to know the difference.'

Assertiveness

In a later chapter we will consider the importance of assertiveness. Assertiveness means insisting on respect for your rights and respecting the rights of other people. If you take time to listen to people, gain their respect and their commitment, then the manager's role will be less stressful as will the approach of the team. Relationships built on mutual respect laced with humour will create a pleasant atmosphere without declining into a sloppy 'clubby' approach.

Environment

Many company directors feel that money spent on making the workplace more attractive is frivolous; and yet they don't begrudge money spent on decorating their homes. An attractive office or factory has a positive impact on the people who work there and thus reduces stress. If thrifty chairmen object to spending money on interior decoration, they should try to work out the cost of time lost due to stress-related disease. If this bill can be reduced then even on purely economic grounds there is a case for spending, apart from grounds of humanity and enhanced motivation.

Balanced life

Your mother probably told you that all work and no play makes Jack a dull boy and she was right. There must be a three-way balance in life between work, home and leisure. The three factors are all important and if one is missing completely, the manager will find life out of balance. The workaholic will find that the stress created by ignoring home life will ultimately have a detrimental impact on effectiveness at work; likewise a tedious job can create home problems, as the worker comes home unfulfilled and resentful. Both men and women need leisure which should be viewed positively as a means of renewal after work and home.

Exercise and diet

The life of a modern executive is sedentary and over-indulgent. Today's businessman is yesterday's Roman Emperor – overweight and under exercised. The cost to com-

panies of heart attacks, bronchitis, strokes, and the other
diseases of the western world are so high that to install a
company gym and to bar sugar and cakes from the canteen
would be paid back in months. Many books have been written
about health and I don't propose to duplicate them. However,
an unhealthy manager is by definition less effective than a
healthy manager, all other things being equal. A strategy for
improved physical effectiveness would be:

- Stop smoking completely

- Exercise vigorously for at least three periods of twenty
  minutes each week. (Always build up to exercise and
  check with your doctor if you have spent years in
  company cars and hotel bars.)

- Watch your diet; cut down on sugar and saturated fat,
  eat more fibre and fresh food.

- Drink alcohol in moderation.

Remember, a dead manager cannot be effective! As well as
keeping alive, sport and exercise increases the ability to relax
and improves the flow of oxygen to the brain, which has a
beneficial effect on thinking skills.

Relaxation
Relaxation is a skill which is rarely taught. Those who can
relax easily never need to think out how they do it; those who
can't are usually too tense to sit down and learn. Many books
set out relaxation techniques and if a manager has a problem
with relaxation, the expenditure of money on the books and
time to reflect on the techniques will generate high returns in
terms of undisturbed sleep, improved personal relationships,
better personal organization and enhanced quality of life.

Facing emotion
It is better to face emotion and release it than to repress it.
Emotional control is important to a manager, decisions made
in anger are rarely effective. However, controlling emotion is
not to repress it; emotion needs an outlet, exercise is often
particularly effective in providing that outlet. Emotion is
energy coursing round the body; without a safety valve the
system explodes.

Self Development Activities

Analyse your management of stress.

> Do you take work home regularly?
> How many hours do you work each week?
> Do you always take your full allowance of holidays?
> Do you smoke?
> How much do you drink?
> How often do you exercise?
> Do you ever have sleepless nights?
> Do you suffer from any of the symptoms of stress?
> If you do, what causes this stress? What can you do to remove the cause?
> How do you use your leisure time?

Then, consider your staff.

> Do your staff work long hours?
> Do they need to work long hours?
> Are all your demands for information reasonable?
> Have you recognized any signs of stress in them?
> Do you stop them if you see them taking work home?

11
Self Development

Before moving on to consider your relationships with other people, I want to encourage you to take a look at yourself. When we look at training, coaching and motivating, I shall be considering the importance of these activities in the management of people. But first, it is important to consider your own development: I believe that a manager who does not want to develop himself will not develop other people. If you've reached your plateau and are no longer interested in growing as a manager, you will find it difficult to instil enthusiasm and commitment into your staff. How many managers have retired at forty and are just waiting for the company to retire them at sixty-five? If you are reading this book, it is unlikely that you are one of them but be warned – once you stop growing in management, you will not keep still – you'll sink.

Why should you maintain an interest in self development?

- It is no longer possible to learn a business and then sit back, knowing everything. Today's world changes rapidly and although you may be a market leader today, tomorrow's new products and new technology may be waiting to pull you out of the spotlight. You need to keep a keen awareness of the world that you work in, otherwise it may change when you're out on your coffee break.

- Development is natural. People only stop developing when barriers are put in their way. The barriers to self development are self-imposed. These barriers can vary from laziness through arrogance to the 'I'm paid to do a job and no more' approach. People who want to enjoy their work don't spent their lives fighting off change but anticipate it and keep ahead of it.

- Ambition has had a bad press since the Macbeths killed Duncan. It is, in fact, an extremely healthy emotion provided that it is kept under control. If you always keep your eyes on your boss's job, you will find yourself tripping up in your current job. But, if nobody wants the senior jobs then the company's management development programme will be so much wasted time. If you want promotion, then work out what you need to do to get it – short of tampering with the brakes on the boss's Jaguar.

Know Thyself

The oracle at Delphi was alleged to have 'Know Thyself' engraved nearby. Before we start to deal with other people and especially before we manage them, we need to know ourselves intimately and objectively. Managing yourself is at least as difficult as managing other people, often more difficult. To avoid endless aimless soul searching, limit your self-appraisal to three main areas:

Strengths
What are you good at? This is no time to be modest. List the skills and knowledge that you possess. This should have three effects:

- You will be surprised at how good you are and you will certainly develop confidence as a result.

- You will begin to understand how you can use those strengths in your current job.

- You may also begin to see how you can use those strengths either in a future position or in anticipating future problems.

Compare your strengths to the main characteristics which are required for your job now and in the future or for any more senior jobs that you aspire to.

Weaknesses
What are you not so good at? How does that affect your job?

How will it affect you in the future? Set yourself goals to improve and if possible recruit people to work for you whose strengths complement your weaknesses. A team that is staffed from strength will be a more effective team than one which just avoids weaknesses.

Learning style
How do you learn best? Do you learn by doing, talking or reading? Think this out carefully so that you can make the best use of learning opportunities when they come along and so you can put yourself in a position where you can learn most effectively.

A Few More Ideas

- Keep up to date in both your specialism and in management techniques generally. Always read trade papers, go to exhibitions, read quality newspapers and watch current affairs programmes on TV. Try to spot trends and be ready for them. Be aware and alert for opportunities.

- Learn to review projects and tasks regularly. Much of the really effective learning goes on by reflecting on experience gained: reviewing the good things so that they can be repeated and reviewing the bad things so that they can be avoided. It is true that experience is the best teacher but only when it is reviewed systematically.

- Ask your boss at appraisal time to tell you what you do well and not so well. Ask what you need to be doing in the future and how your abilities match those required by your organization in the future. If they don't match, then don't spend years forcing yourself to work in an unnatural way; you will be unhappy and you can never be 100 per cent schizophrenic. Find a company who wants what you have to offer.

- Plan your career. My work involves running assessment centres for managers and then planning training programmes to allow them to achieve their potential and fill senior positions. In my experience, the manager who has thought out his career in advance is as rare as a white rhinoceros. Don't wait for your organization to plan your career for you; make your own plans. They will be particularly impressed and you will achieve what you want to achieve and will use your strengths to the full.

- Use the self development activities in this book to think about your performance as a manager. All the skills in the book are needed to be fully effective.

The critical theme in self development is that you must make your career reflect your strengths and not just stumble along. Good managers develop until they drop, learning new things and finding new abilities. By continually developing themselves, they continue to develop everyone else.

12
Communication

Communication is a word which has lost some of its value because of over-use. Every management trainer is told to run a course on communication at some time and it crops up on appraisal forms with monotonous regularity. Nevertheless, it is an important concept, too important to be left out of a book like this. If this chapter seems too thin, it is because I have taken up the communication issue elsewhere in the book. Communication is a critical element in decision-making, leadership, discipline, coaching and so on. It is more sensible to consider it an integral part of other activities than as an activity on its own. After all, we don't decide just to communicate; we only communicate when we have something to say.

We need to think carefully, though, before we communicate. The modern organization is filled with communication and before we add to that, we need to stand back and think whether it will be effective communication.

Why?

Why communicate at all?

- To inform. Information is the bread and butter of the modern organization. Without information organizations couldn't function effectively.

- To educate. The more people know about the business, the more effective they will be. We should aim to develop people by telling them more than the basic information that they need just to carry out their job.

- To motivate. One of the biggest diseconomies of scale in

the modern organization is that people become so
specialized that they never see the end product of their
labour. If people understand why they are doing things,
they will be able to adapt their work more consciously
to that end product.

What?

Without developing an exhaustive or exhausting list, there are
certain categories of information which should be communicated. It is almost equally important to decide what
shouldn't be communicated. Briefing sessions every day soon
lose their impetus and become tedious to everyone. The test of
good communication is: *Will it help them to do their job
better?*

So, you should be clarifying:

- The aims of the team and the individual.

- The main responsibilities of an individual's job.

- The full terms and conditions of employment.

- Information about the department – results, newly
  appointed staff, costs and profitability.

- Company results and new developments.

- Information about an individual's own performance
  and future progression.

- Company policies which affect staff.

- How to work safely and effectively.

- What happens to work when it leaves their department.

- How customers react to the product.

The what-nots. The things not to communicate:

- Subjective information which is founded on rumour.

- Premature information which may cause unrest and
  insecurity.

- Information on obscure company policies which has no
  relevance.

- Information in which the cost of research outweighs the benefit to the receiver.

Who by and to Whom?

Communication is not just by a manager to his team. It can be by any manager to any group of staff: the production manager to shop stewards; the personnel manager to any group of people and so on. All managers are responsible for their own staff and also for making sure that information about their area is communicated in every direction necessary. The safety officer hears about new health and safety legislation – he should make sure that the people who need to know, *do* know.

To whom? Remember, 'Will it help them to do their job better?' If you have information which can make people more effective, then pass it on. Think about your audience, it will help you to answer the next question.

How?

Think about the purpose of your communication. Then consider the audience. What is their level of knowledge? What do they need to know? Is this likely to be sensitive? Will they need to ask questions?

Consider the options open to you but remember:

- Aim for clarity and brevity.

- If you want to use statistics, make sure that you have some supporting notes. People can't digest figures at one sitting.

- Don't hide behind vindictive memos.

- Give the opportunity for a response where possible. Communication is a two-way channel.

- Announce controversial decisions face-to-face. If you're well briefed and honest, you should have no problems. If you are not either of these, why are you making the decision?

- Use more than one method if necessary – for example, an oral briefing can be backed up by a written notice.

When?

Communicate important messages before they start to course around the grapevine. But beware Catch 22 of communications – the denial. If you deny a rumour then everyone will say, 'They're denying it – there must be something in it.' But, if you don't deny a rumour then the cognoscenti will say, 'You notice they're not denying it.'

Try not to deny but announce something that will scotch the rumour by implication. For instance, you may combat an unfounded rumour of a factory closure by announcing to the staff the development of a new product. Don't be too close in your timing, otherwise people will see something in the announcement that isn't there.

Plan the timing of announcements, especially if they have industrial relations implications or are likely to be of interest to the press. Try to arrange for all interested parties to be briefed simultaneously. Even geography is no protection – I've heard of American staff ringing British newspapers with company news relating to their British counterparts. I've even heard of American unions ringing through to their British brothers before the British managing director knew. This can happen in microcosm in your department.

Where?

Get people together at their workplace, not yours. Ask the lads from the factory into your plush office and they will be ill at ease and defensive. There is more informal communication than formal and you should be communicating regularly at the workplace. Two-way communication is more natural there and is far more beneficial.

Self Development Activities

1   Go down to the shop-floor or store or warehouse and start to ask questions about the job. See what your staff understand and what they don't. These are valuable clues for your next briefing session.

2   Could your department benefit from a higher profile? Do people know what your team does and can do for them? If not, have you failed to communicate clearly? Plan to rectify this.

13
Dealing with Other People

The majority of the inmates in the Home for Bewildered Managers are there because of the problems they have in forming relationships with people. This is not necessarily because they are sociopathic or pure misfits; they are often there because they have been confused by management trainers and psychologists. Many of the trendy courses on man management have taken managers away from their natural instincts. What is it that work does to people? The woman who is a good mother to her children and a good daughter to her parents becomes the harridan of the data processing room. The chap who plays a good set of darts and is too timid to effect a decent tackle on the rugby pitch becomes a cold-hearted destroyer of careers.

The people that we work with are just that – people. They don't just bring a briefcase and a thermos flask to work; they bring emotions, prejudices, fears and hopes. So do we. We expect to be treated with civility and respect; so do they. We are all a complex bundle of egos and ids with needs for status, affection and dominance. Yet we all have to work together, to overcome these barriers and get on with the job.

Let's look at some guidelines for effective working with people in organizations:

1 Everyone has certain rights – to be treated with respect, to be listened to carefully and to defend themselves against unwarranted criticism, for example. If organizations are going to function smoothly, then those rights must be respected by everyone. Many managers who are decent, courteous people at home turn into raging psychopaths at work and create havoc by turning every meeting into a showdown.

2 Everyone also has a right to assert themselves or not.

Assertiveness is not just a question of insisting on your rights without being aggressive or submissive; it is a way of bringing matters out into the open without allowing them to become out of hand. Assertiveness should be a way of life for all adults as it is an adult form of behaviour. Vulgar aggression which is offensive and dysfunctional belongs in the school playground not in the office or factory. So does timidity and submissiveness – as managers we should have the guts to stand up for our own rights and the rights of our team. Next time that you are in a meeting, look for the bully and look for the jelly, what is the effect of their behaviour? Remember what your mother told you – 'stand up (i.e. be assertive) to the bully and they will always back down.'

3   Everyone has the right to be listened to carefully. Effective listening is much more than just being silent when somebody speaks, it consists of:

- *Hearing* – Make sure that you are in a position to hear what people are saying.

- *Watching* – Look for clues in the gestures they make. This will tell you how they really feel about the subject.

- *Understanding* – Make sure that you understand what people are saying. If it is not clear, don't make assumptions but ask for clarification.

- *Recording* – If you need to, write key notes to yourself so that you remember what was said.

- *Looking* – Don't just listen, look as though you are listening. You learn more by listening than talking; so try to encourage the talker by looking interested.

4   Be aware of your own emotions and prejudices. Do you have a short fuse? If so, make sure that you make your points clearly before you begin to lose your temper. Do you give way under pressure? If so, work hard at presenting your case clearly and assertively, anticipating any likely objections.

What is the main obstruction when you are trying to deal with people? Once you have clarified that, you will find it easier to avoid situations when it can get in the way.

5   If you feel that emotions are at stake, confront them early before they explode into conflict. Both parties in a communication have a responsibility to do this. Disagreements are a healthy and desirable part of a manager's life, but when they spill over into conflict they become unhealthy and undesirable. Conflict is caused when something that we value is threatened and we react defensively. The emphasis changes from solving the problem under discussion to winning a battle. In a conflict, the losses to both sides are usually much larger than their gains. Nobody wins a war apart from the armament manufacturers, nobody wins an industrial dispute apart from your competitors and nobody wins an interdepartmental dispute apart from the man or woman holding the coats.

The rest of this section is looking at our dealings with people – people who may have ambitions, prejudices, mortgages, hangovers, middle-aged spread, pre-menstrual tension and halitosis. They are not automata and neither are you; remember that as you read on.

Self Development Activities

1   At the next meeting you attend, concentrate on listening carefully and note down what people say. What did you learn? Did you find it difficult to resist butting in?

2   List the things people do which annoy you.
   Make a list of the things you do which you think may irritate other people.
   Consider your prejudices – are there any types of people whom you automatically dislike?

3   Think back to an event when you either:
   a) disregarded someone's feelings
       or
   b) failed to assert yourself.
   What caused it?
   What were the effects?
   How would you respond in future?

14
Presenting your Case

Consider these two scenarios.

Scene One

One of the world's leading experts on a particular co-polymer of polyethylene is trying to sell an idea to Worldchem, the world's largest chemical company. Turning to the blackboard which he covers with obscure formulae, he talks quickly and quietly in a strong middle European accent describing by mathematics how he came to make the discovery of this new plastic. Two hours later his audience, mainly American financiers, are confused and tired. They turn down his proposal, preferring to move on to an interesting presentation from a local research centre which although technically inferior is at least clear, concise and comprehensible. The professor, mortified, commits suicide. As his epitaph they wrote, 'He forgot whom he was talking to.'

Scene Two

Pitching for a new account, the advertising agency prepare a presentation for their potential clients, baked bean manufacturers. They use video, tapes, flashing slides, mock-ups of the product and tele-ads and present the clients with beautifully bound copies of the presentation along with a folder of photographs. The presentation takes place at a London hotel with smoked salmon, champagne cocktails, caviar and, of course, baked beans. The highspot of the presentation is dancing girls bursting out of a tin of baked beans singing the jingle for the advert. The chairman of the baked bean producers asks, 'Can we have some costings for your proposals?' The agency men look at each other and say, 'Well, not really. We've still got some work to do on that.' The moral: prepare the content as well as the delivery.

The delivery and the content are of equal importance in making a presentation. The presenter is not just transmitting facts to the listener, he is trying to persuade them to buy the product, accept the recommendation, assimilate the information. In short, the presenter wants the commitment of the listener. This is not done by a turgid litany of fact and statistics; it is also not done by attempting to mask poor content by extravagant presentation. It is done by preparing both the case and the presentation and by delivering it in an effective and confident way. Many managers with a fine technical grasp of their subject fail to make that apparent by presenting it badly. Presentation skills can be taught like any other.

Preparing a Presentation

Step 1 — What is your message?
Write down the main points that you want to get over in the presentation. Write the key points down and then put them down in a logical order. Make sure that you don't take great logical leaps and that information is placed before conclusions. Use brainstorming to generate ideas, if necessary.

Step 2 — Who are your audience?
The mistake that the professor made in scene one was to forget to direct his message towards his audience. Consider:

- Who are the audience?

- What do they know about your subject?

- What will they be expecting from your presentation?

- What do you expect from them? — a decision, acceptance of your recommendations, a burst of spontaneous applause?

- How long are they prepared to let you speak?

- Are they likely to be hostile or friendly?

- What information will they need to make a decision?

The answer to these questions should clarify the purpose of your presentation and set the tone for your preparatory work.

Step 3 — Plan the structure of your presentation
Now you are starting to do the detailed work. You should be clear about what you want to say and whom you want to say it to. This step takes care of the when, where and how. Do not over-complicate. Think about your presentation having a beginning, a middle and an end and you start to break it into easy chunks, so that you are not trying to plan the whole thing at once.

Beginning: Plan to start your presentation with a clear statement of purpose. Explain who you are and why you are making the presentation. Explain the structure of the presentation and when you will be prepared to accept questions. You will need to emphasize this, it helps you to establish control over the audience; after all, who is giving this presentation? You should also use the beginning to emphasize to your audience the benefits of listening to your presentation.

Middle: Make sure that the main part of your presentation is both concise and logical. Place your key points in a logical order and only include facts which are relevant to those points. Try to stop your key points from running into each other; they are discrete points in your case and the audience needs to be clear when you have finished one and are moving on to another.

End: Be ready to include a summary. The summary must be even better planned than the rest of the presentation because it is more likely to be listened to than any other part. Vicars and priests will tell you of the Pavlovian reaction from congregations to the word 'finally'. Use the summary not as a run down to the end but as a re-emphasis of the key points. If there is a sales pitch, plan to put it in there. If you want something from your audience, leave them very clear what it is.

Step 4 — Plan your visual aids
Visual aids can enhance your message. They can also draw attention away from it, so plan them carefully. The purpose of a visual aid is to underline and not to obscure. If your audience leaves remembering the visual aids but not the message then you have not planned them effectively. The advertising

agency in scene two put more emphasis on the visual aids than the content and failed. Consider the following points:

- Don't crowd a visual aid. Use two simple slides in place of one complex one.

- If you need statistics in a presentation, be selective about which ones you use and make sure that there is always some way of showing them to your audience.

- When you are not referring to a visual aid remove it; it will either confuse or distract.

- Make sure all visual aids are visible and legible throughout the room.

- Murphy's Law of Presentations says, 'The likelihood of a visual aid going wrong increases in direct proportion to its importance to the presentation.' If the visual aid is vital, ensure you have a back-up.

- By all means give handouts but not until the end of your presentation – otherwise the audience will read them instead of listening to you. If the handout is more interesting than you are, you shouldn't be the one to make the presentation.

- Vary your visual aids – but not too much. Flip-charts, overhead slides, maps, videos, cassettes, tape/slides, 16 mm slides, films, models, examples of products, photographs and so on are all available to the presenter. I repeat, use them to underline and not to obscure.

Step 5 — Transfer your talk on to notes

Unless you are very confident, you will probably want to use notes. Make them unobtrusive. Post-cards are ideal for key points, preferably with emphatic points written in red or green. Don't write the whole talk down; reading a presentation is hopelessly boring for both you and your audience. Put key points down and rehearse a little or a lot according to taste.

Step 6 — Check the room

Check the room, visual aids and layout of tables before you make the presentation. Make sure everyone can see and that the table layout is appropriate for the level of audience participation you require. Auditorium seating in rows inhibits audience discussion; a horseshoe or rectangle encourages it.

Delivering the Presentation

The presenter has to be part actor and actually perform for the audience. The performance must underline the message, not obscure it. A presentation which is a string of anecdotes and jokes may be amusing but will the audience go away remembering your message? Conversely, if you deliver the presentation like a Russian newscaster, you will obscure your message by boring everyone to tears.

A good delivery uses the whole body and not just the mouth.

Eyes: Watch your audience, not the back of the room or your feet. Audiences give very clear signals to the speaker about their reaction to what you are saying. Yawning, shuffling, frowning and grimacing are all signs to the alert speaker. Also, making eye contact with your audience gives a presentation a personal element and you should spread your eye contact around. *Don't* deliver your talk to the senior manager present – it will prevent him from nodding off and will irritate his acolytes immensely.

Voice: The voice is a delicate instrument. It can emphasize, amuse, motivate, inspire and enthuse. That is why we watch or listen to a play rather than read it. A presenter should use the voice to the extent of its performance. Vary pace and volume to make your delivery more interesting. Emphasize key words and phrases and avoid a dreary monotone at all costs.

Hands: There are two extremes to avoid in using hand gestures. Extravagant gestures which involve waving your arms like an aerobics student are likely to distract the audience. At the other end of the scale, standing like a skittle in an alley, arms pinned to the side or, even worse, the genital clutch, beloved of footballers, are both only likely to make people think you are a robot and not a presenter. Gestures can be helpful but not too many or too eccentric.

Feet: You don't have to be welded to the lectern, nor is it advisable to go walkabout. If you are wearing a tie microphone, find out how long the lead is and try to regard that as the outer radius of your wanderings!

Ten Ways to Distract an Audience

If you really want to irritate or distract your audience, here are ten helpful hints.

1   Rattle the loose change in your pocket.

2   Smoke while you are presenting. There is bound to be one non-smoker in the audience and it will really annoy them.

3   Take regular sips of water or coffee. This is really annoying if your audience haven't been given anything to drink.

4   Start most sentences with 'OK' or 'basically'.

5   Use 'Y'know' and 'kinda' to link thoughts within a sentence.

6   When you write on a flip-chart, try to talk into it. Paper is useful for deadening sound.

7   If you are using a microphone, don't test it beforehand. Pick it up just before you speak and say 'one, two, three, four – testing, testing' into it.

8   If a car goes past or a 'plane flies over, don't stop talking. Audiences can lip-read and they enjoy the challenge of working out what you said during the noisy interval.

9   Try to make as many offensive jokes as possible. That way you increase the likelihood of irritating at least someone.

10   If you are making a presentation to managers from another organization, try to make some facetious comments about their products or their business. This is even more effective if you want to sell something to them. Managers love to deal with humorists.

The Impromptu Presentation

If you are asked to speak at very short notice, follow the following drill:

1   Stay calm.

2   Write some key points on a card.

3   Use a flip-chart to cover any statistics or facts that need to be seen rather than heard.

4   Keep your comments brief. Try not to ramble on, a typical reaction to an impromptu invitation to speak.

5   Don't say 'at such short notice it is difficult to say too much'. People will know that it's at short notice and you will gain more kudos from a calm delivery than a whingeing excuse.

Self Development Activities

1   Use a cassette recorder to rehearse presentations, at least at first. Listen to your inflections and emphasis.

2   Try to persuade someone to video one of your present-ations. Then watch it alone and note down the good and bad points. Be as critical as you can but don't be demoralized; eveyone looks worse to themselves than they do to other people.

3   Watch other presenters critically. What do they do that illuminates their message and what obscures it?

15
Learners and Trainers

Learning is a process which never stops. We start to learn in the womb and we continue to learn until we die. Learning is something that we can't help doing because we are human beings with a strong desire to survive, so we adapt to changing circumstances in a way that will enhance our chances of keeping going for a little longer. When we were children we learnt that doing certain things would result in pain and doing other things would result in pleasure. Throughout our lives we seek to avoid the one and maximize the other.

There are a few conclusions that stem from this:

- People learn all the time. We, as managers, must ensure that they learn the right things and not the wrong things.

- Learning is not confined to the inside of a classroom, it is carried out wherever people live and work. The world of work is full of opportunities to learn; we have to make sure that we use them.

- As managers, we are able to give carrots and wield sticks – pay, promotion, interesting work, pleasant working conditions and so on. Thus we have a similar role in the learning process of our staff as a parent to their children. By thanking people for work of a particular standard and haranguing them for work of inferior quality, we are teaching them the standards which are acceptable to us. By pouring scorn on new ideas and rewarding the same tired old solutions to new problems, we are teaching our staff that creative thinking doesn't pay.

- Learning is most effective when the learner is motivated. This motivation is usually related to the pleasure and pain principle. The perception of this relationship is particularly important, thus you should make sure that the learner understands the purpose of any learning sessions. The more closely the learning event relates to improving or protecting the learner's position, the more effective the learning will be.

Most managers agree that experience is the best teacher and this is true. Based on the view that we are always learning, many years at work are bound to be more fruitful than a week at a training course, however intensive the experience. Training courses are also a way of learning by experience – the experience of others, distilled and put over by a professional presenter. The effective manager examines this experience, compares it with his own and retains those parts which seem to help, discarding those parts which do not.

Experience is only the best teacher under certain circumstances:

- That twenty years' experience is just that and not one year's experience multiplied by twenty.

- That experience is reviewed and reflected upon. A good way of reviewing is to consider after each activity –
  — Did I achieve my purpose? If so, why? If not, why not?
  — What went well in the activity? How can I make sure that I do that again?
  — What went badly? How can I prevent it happening again?

- That the learner is encouraged to test out new concepts and review them.

- That both teacher and learner are alert to learning opportunities. The range of opportunities in working life are immense. The organization should be the manager's play-pen, full of things which stimulate learning, to examine and test. By observing other people carefully; how they handle particular situations and how they work, we can learn not only from our experience but from theirs. Organizations where people are all learning from each other are interesting and exciting places to be.

Manager as Trainer

Not everything can be left to experience. Some skills and knowledge are passed on more effectively by a skilled trainer, summarizing and presenting them to the learner. Without training, we would all have had to learn quite basic skills from scratch. If no one had taught us to tie a shoelace as children, we would all have developed our own way of doing it but much later in life. We train our staff for a variety of reasons.

- To prevent the manager from doing every task himself.

- To spread the best practice in the organization.

- To reduce the time in which a member of staff becomes fully effective.

- To improve quality of performance.

- Training increases the job satisfaction of both the trainer and trainee and thus reduces labour turnover, absenteeism and accidents.

Training is a skill like any other. It needs planning systematically, carrying out carefully and evaluating, as follows.

What Training is Needed?

Like learning opportunities, training needs are all around us waiting to be spied by the vigilant manager. Some places in which they can be found:

- The job description. What is the job-holder required to do? Can they do them? If there is a gap, then there is a training need.

- Appraisal forms. Problems which are identified at appraisal time should be regarded as training needs.

- Any of the normal performance indicators should be examined by the manager for they are a rich source of information about training needs, such as:

— A drop in sales can reflect a training need in cold selling, telephone sales, perception of selling opportunities and customer relations.

— A rise in costs can reflect a training need in cost control, energy usage and productivity systems.

— A rise in accidents can indicate a need for training in health and safety.

— High labour turnover can imply a need for better induction training and man-management training for first-line managers.

— A high level of customer complaints can point to a need for training in customer relations, production, distribution or marketing.

Planning a Training Session

The effective manager plans a training session with four important factors in mind.

The aim: Why are you carrying out a training session? What do you hope to achieve by it? What do you want the trainee to be able to do or know at the end of the session? What standards of performance are you expecting to result from the session? How will you measure your own success? By reaction of the trainee or a measurable improvement in performance?

The trainee: What does the trainee know about the subject? What do they need to know? What is their background? How are they likely to feel about the training – cynical, apprehensive, confident? How do they learn best – reading, reflecting or doing? A theoretical approach may be fine for the research chemist but would be a disaster for the human dynamo with a CSE in woodwork. If you are training a group, what is the mix like? How much time will the trainees need to prepare for the session? What is the trainees' attention span?

The method: Combine your thinking on the above with some consideration of the right method. There are many methods available to the trainer, who after considering the aim and the trainee should consider cost, complexity of subject, availability and effectiveness of materials. Some options are: computer based training; a training course; one-to-one instruction; coaching; supervized practice; video; tape-slide machine; and directed reading.

The location: Re-read the chapter on presentation skills and ensure that the venue is conducive to effective learning. Try to protect the trainee from distractions and select the right amount of time for the session.

If you are making a presentation ensure that you have prepared it fully. Even if you know the job backwards, don't just turn up and carry out the session. The greatest expert in any field needs to pass on that expertise in the most effective and systematic way if it is to be useful to the trainee.

Carrying out a Training Session

1 Put the job into context. Never start training just by teaching a process. Start with the whole story and explain why the job has to be done and how it fits into the department's aims and can further the aims of the whole organization. Training checkout operators to operate tills quickly and efficiently has an impact on the customer relations of the store and helps to increase sales – tell them that and even a repetitive task will take on new significance.

Also show trainees the whole process first before turning to the detail of the job. This adds to the trainees' understanding of why things are done in a particular order and, also, where there is discretion to make changes.

2 When considering the detail, break the process down into logical but easily comprehensible parts. It may help to see the training session as a meal. If it is eaten in small mouthfuls, course by course, the diner will enjoy it, taste every mouthful and not feel overfed. If it is bolted down all together, the diner will not be able to differentiate between courses and will also get terrible indigestion. Feed the trainee at an appropriate speed; if the speed is too slow, then quicken up. After each stage, check that the trainee has fully understood before moving on.

3 Allow the trainee time to practice. This enables you to check understanding and allows the trainee to gain confidence before leaving the session. People only learn completely by doing things themselves. The Chinese say, 'I hear and I forget; I see and I remember; I do and I understand.'

4 The trainer should give a regular response to the trainee's efforts, both a response on what the trainee is doing well and on the areas in which improvement is needed. Even

criticism should be positive and addressed in a way that encourages the trainee to improve. Humiliation in a training session is out. How can someone be motivated to learn if you have just completely demoralized them? Their only aim is to get out of the room and die.

5   Leave your ego behind you when you walk into a training room. Your aim is to teach the trainee and not to let them know the extent of your knowledge and the depths of your technical jargon. If you want to improve your reputation in the organization, let your trumpet be blown by your successful trainees and not by you at their expense.

Has your Training been Successful?

If you are to be satisfied with the training you give, you have to evaluate its success. Have you met your aims? In particular, has the trainees' performance improved? This is easy to assess in training factory operators but very hard in training managers, because the manager's performance is in isolation more difficult to evaluate.

Self Development Activities

1   Write down all the things that you learn in any day you choose. Write down all the things that people have learned from you – formally and informally.

2   List any learning opportunities in your area of responsibility. Can you use them to learn or to teach?

3   List the training needs in your area. Plan to satisfy them as soon as possible.

16
Interviewing

The interview is the setting for many of the critical incidents in the relationship between managers and staff – recruitment, appraisal, grievance and disciplinary action. The benefits of managing those interviews correctly are immense – matched only by the costs of getting them wrong. If our staff come to us for an interview and feel that we are unprepared and prejudiced, they will leave dissatisfied and demotivated. If they find us well-briefed and prepared to listen and question positively, they are more likely to leave committed to the conclusion of the interview.

A little thought about the way you carry out an interview and the development of some skills can transform your interviews from problems into opportunities. There are some skills which are general interviewing skills; others are specific to particular types of interview. First, some general points.

- Interviews are like operas, they use both words and music. The words are the questions and answers, the music is the atmosphere of the interview. Both are equally important; saying the right thing in the wrong way is almost as bad as saying the wrong thing.

- Interviews are stressful for both parties. Stress can be reduced by adequate preparation and by creating the right atmosphere.

- Work hard at your interviewing manner. Leave the interviewee thinking about their performance and not yours.

Preparing for Interviews

Think about:

- *The purpose.* What is the interview intended to achieve? This is particularly important in interviews related to grievances or disciplinary action. Don't allow a disciplinary interview to be turned into a grievance interview by a cunning interviewee and don't allow yourself to turn an appraisal into a disciplinary interview. Neither of these things will happen if you clarify the purpose.

- *The interviewee – your 'audience'.* What are they like? Confident, timid, aggressive? How will they react to what you are saying?

- *Information.* What information do you need for the interview? Make sure that you have done your homework before the interview and have any information that you need ready to hand.

- *The environment.* Make sure that you are not disturbed. There is no greater sign of unprofessionalism than a manager who is interrupted constantly during his interview – it is discourteous and disruptive. Also, make sure that the seating is right for the purpose. Sitting on a huge chair behind a large desk may be appropriate for a disciplinary interview; it is certainly inappropriate for an appraisal.

- *Your approach.* Sketch out your approach and the main points you wish to make. Then consider the likely response and how you will handle it. Don't be too rigid in sticking to this agenda but to go into an interview without a plan will certainly ensure that you fail to achieve your purpose. Also think carefully about the amount of direction that you will need to exert. Different types of interview require more or less direction than others (See Figure 1).

Carrying out Interviews

First, set the scene. Explain the purpose and the structure of the interview. Tell them how you intend to approach the session

Figure 1 Scale of Direction Provided by Interviewer

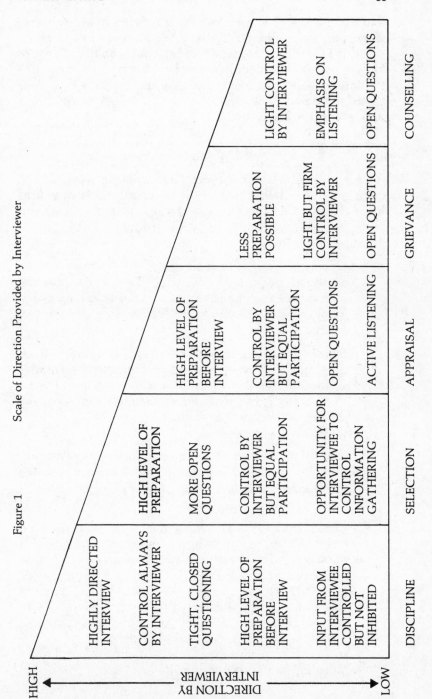

	DISCIPLINE	SELECTION	APPRAISAL	GRIEVANCE	COUNSELLING
	HIGHLY DIRECTED INTERVIEW	HIGH LEVEL OF PREPARATION	HIGH LEVEL OF PREPARATION BEFORE INTERVIEW		LIGHT CONTROL BY INTERVIEWER
	CONTROL ALWAYS BY INTERVIEWER	MORE OPEN QUESTIONS	CONTROL BY INTERVIEWER BUT EQUAL PARTICIPATION	LESS PREPARATION POSSIBLE	EMPHASIS ON LISTENING
	TIGHT, CLOSED QUESTIONING	CONTROL BY INTERVIEWER BUT EQUAL PARTICIPATION	OPEN QUESTIONS	LIGHT BUT FIRM CONTROL BY INTERVIEWER	OPEN QUESTIONS
	HIGH LEVEL OF PREPARATION BEFORE INTERVIEW	OPPORTUNITY FOR INTERVIEWEE TO CONTROL INFORMATION GATHERING	ACTIVE LISTENING	OPEN QUESTIONS	
	INPUT FROM INTERVIEWEE CONTROLLED BUT NOT INHIBITED				

HIGH ← DIRECTION BY INTERVIEWER → LOW

and use the first few minutes to create the right atmosphere. Generally, you will be trying to get the interviewee to relax; you don't want them to feel too constrained and then clam up. However, don't make the interview too laid back; it may make the interviewee so relaxed that they don't perform at their best. Interviewing consists of two actions – asking questions and listening to the answers.

Asking Questions

As any lover of TV police procedural dramas knows, asking questions in the right way is a skill. Asking the right questions in the right way will accrue far better results than asking them in the wrong way. Firstly, let's look at some helpful ways of phrasing questions.

- *Open questions.* These are questions which cannot be answered by just 'yes' or 'no'. They encourage the interviewee to expand on the topic. For example, ask 'How did you feel about that?' rather than 'Did you feel angry?'

- *Simple interrogatives.* These are extremely open questions and are very useful probing supplementaries – How? Why? When? Why not? The essence of good questioning is to probe answers skilfully and not take the first answer at face value.

- *Reflective questions.* If you don't understand an answer, the reflective question summarizes what you thought you heard and checks that summary with the interviewee. This is a useful way of clarifying blurred edges.

- *Closed questions.* The evasive interviewee can take a series of open questions as an invitation to talk around the subject. The effective interviewer can bring a halt to a circumlocutary answer by asking a short closed question, that is a question which can be answered by 'yes' or 'no'. It is quite likely that the crafty interviewee will continue to evade, so you must be prepared to repeat the question. Look at this example:
  MANAGER: Can you explain what happened on Friday morning? (an open question).

INTERVIEWEE: Well, it was very difficult. What with my wife off sick and the children to get off to school . . . *(ten minutes elapse)*. . . so it was all very difficult.
MANAGER: But were you late? (a closed question)
INTERVIEWEE: The trains were on strike that day and –
MANAGER: But were you late?
INTERVIEWEE: Yes.

There are also some types of question which don't help.

- *Leading questions.* These are questions which suggest a particular answer. They are always stopped by High Court judges on TV and in real life.

- *Trick questions.* Trying to be too clever, especially in appraisal or disciplinary interviews, can be counter-productive; it will only make the interviewee defensive.

- *Marathon questions.* Avoid lengthy or complex questions. If the question is unclear the answer will be ambiguous.

- *Discriminatory questions.* Make sure that you know the law before you carry out a recruitment interview and don't ask questions which discriminate on grounds of race, religion or sex.

- *Closed questions.* Yes, I know I said they were helpful but only in their place. Out of place they allow the interviewee to answer in monosyllables.

Listening to the Answers

Listen actively. That is:

- Look interested.

- Probe and clarify the answers you are given.

- Make notes for retention later but explain the purpose of the notes.

- Make encouraging noises. Greeting answers with silence is a technique that went out with the ark.

Finishing and Following Up

End the interview with a summary of the course of action that you intend to take and any commitments that the trainee has made. (So, in a disciplinary interview, agree the standard required, action to be taken to meet that standard, how it will be monitored and a time for review.)

Then, make sure you carry out your part of the agreement and don't regard the end of the interview as the end of the business. The interviewing process is not over until you have done everything you contracted to do at the interview.

Some specific types of interview need particular skills:

The Selection Interview

The important stage in selection interviewing is preparation. Before even looking at application forms, the recruiter must be very clear about the job which is to be filled and the type of candidate who is needed to fill it. These are the measures against which to compare the applicants. Eliminate those who don't meet your essential requirements in terms of experience and qualifications. Then carry out your interviews.

Selection is a two-way process. The candidate needs to understand the job and the conditions attached to it, you need to assess the candidate. Build in time to explain what the job entails and any company information you think is necessary.

Remember the 'halo' and 'horns' effects. These are two perspectives of the same philosophy. Every unwary manager recruits staff in the way God made Adam – in his own image. We are drawn to people like ourselves and when we see similarities in, say, education or hobbies, we subconsciously allow this to colour our perception of the candidate (the halo effect). The reverse holds for interests which differ from ours (the horns effect). The halo effect is not just stereotyping. Because we have a shared interest we are more likely to have a more relaxed chat at the beginning of the interview and thus the candidate will seem more confident and articulate. The opposite holds for the horns effect.

The Appraisal Interview

Many companies encourage annual appraisal interviews.

Without training or preparation these can be a disaster. Done properly, they are of great benefit. These are some guidelines:

- Review the whole year's performance, not just yesterday's.

- Prepare carefully. Read last year's appraisal notes, plan your approach, be clear about the points you want to make.

- Start the interview on a positive note. Review the good points before the bad. Review the bad points with improvement in mind, not humiliation.

- Agree an action plan and ensure that it is recorded.

- Don't avoid problem areas but approach them positively. Don't turn an appraisal into a disciplinary interview.

- Use the interview to motivate. Set new and challenging goals and send the interviewee out ready to achieve them.

- Review these goals regularly. Appraise regularly – don't leave things until the 'annual ordeal'.

The Disciplinary Interview

Discipline is such an important part of a manager's job that I have given it a whole chapter (chapter 23). The interview is likely to be stressful for both parties. The interviewer has to cut through the emotion to analyse the problem and agree a solution.

- Information gathering is essential. Think about your case and the likely response. Remember that good barristers only ask questions in court to which they already know the answer.

- Keep calm. Don't be swayed by anger, tears, rancour or threats of resignation. Beware of the worst type of all – the plea-bargainer, the person who owns up quickly to avoid the worst of the retribution.

- Agree an action plan and a review time.

The Grievance Interview

The grievance interview can be difficult to prepare for and deal with. Why?

- The 'griever' may be angry, inarticulate or both.

- The ostensive grievance may be only a symptom of a more important problem. This problem may be revealed only under patient and probing questioning.

- Some grievances may be spontaneous and the interviewer may be in a position of carrying out the interview before they are aware that an interview is taking place.

Listen carefully to the grievance. Ask gently probing questions; a grievance, like a boil, may explode under aggressive probing. Don't be rushed into responding immediately but agree a time to meet again and be sure to stick to that agreement. Time does not heal a grievance, it only aggravates it.

The Counselling Interview

Counselling is an advisory role, where a manager may be discussing a work or personal problem with a subordinate. It is a non-directive interview, where the initiative comes from the subordinate. The interviewer is not directing the interview and so the approach is very different from the previous examples. Some pointers to help handle this type of interview:

- Listen carefully and actively.

- Use reflective questions to summarize the story that you hear from the individual. This helps to clarify the problem in both your mind and theirs.

- Avoid giving direct advice. Remember that you are helping them solve the problem and not solving it for them. If you want to give direction, do it by asking carefully phrased questions.

Self Development Activities

1   If you are unsure of your interview technique, arrange to

carry out an interview with an experienced interviewer. Observe their questioning techniques carefully.

2 Take an opportunity to attend an interviewing course which uses video techniques. Watch out for mannerisms and unhelpful questions.

3 Watch TV policemen or barristers. Listen to their question phrasing. John Mortimer's Rumpole and P.D. James's Adam Dalgleish ask beautifully structured questions.

Postscript — on Being Interviewed

1 Dress smartly and arrive on time. To fail to do either of these makes you feel uncomfortable and you will be unable to do yourself justice.

2 Think what questions you would ask if you were the interviewer, then consider the answers you would give if they were put to you.

3 Listen carefully to the questions and try not to answer in monosyllables. An interview is an opportunity to create an impression; a stream of one word answers only gives the impression of an inarticulate moron.

4 Carry out promptly actions that may be required of you after the interview.

17
Getting the Most out of Your Meetings

It is ten-fifteen. The agenda said 10 a.m. Unfortunately the manager who called the meeting still has the agendas on a pile on the table, ready to give them out as people drift in. Three people arrived on time, saw that the meeting was not under-way and wandered off to find the coffee and cigarette machines. The chairman sits rather sheepishly waiting for people to arrive. He begins to stop people leaving the room and so by ten-thirty, there are enough people to make a start.

He hands out the agenda and the minutes of the previous meeting (six weeks ago). He wrote them last night at home. The meeting starts with a protracted bickering about the minutes of the last meeting and drifts on until lunch. After lunch, there is a period of post-prandial torpor until a combination of boredom and frustration drives the parti-cipants into a display of acrimony on some trivial points at the end of the meeting. They all storm out, leaving the chairman to write some minutes out of a tangled mess of decisions and half-decisions. If the whole thing were written by Shakespeare it would be a tragedy.

Meetings have a tremendous potential for achieving high quality work. They can also be a time-wasting bore. Yet, very few companies train people in making their meetings more effective, even though many managers spend half their work-ing lives in attending meetings, preparing for them and recovering from them.

Have you ever costed your meetings? Consider this list for your own meetings:

Travel costs.
Accommodation costs.
Manpower costs.

The cost of the time of the participants is an important factor. This factor can be described in an equation, which I have modestly called 'Lockett's Law'.

$$£WT = ET \times P \times £H$$

where

£WT	=	Total cost of the working time used.
ET	=	Elapsed time.
P	=	Participants at the meeting.
£H	=	The average hourly pay of the participants.

Example

A meeting of eight salesmen (average hourly pay = £7.50) for four hours costs:

$$£240 = 8 \times 4 \times 7.5$$

This cost of £240 does not include welfare costs or any other employment costs. Nor does it include preparation time, debriefing time or time for carrying out the agreed action. Calling a meeting can become more expensive than ordering a piece of capital equipment and yet it is done with far less thought.

The Purpose of the Meeting

Why are you calling a meeting? Clarify this immediately. This simple question should set the agenda, the number of participants and the likely end result.

For example, you decide to call a meeting to discuss the launching of a new product. Is it to make decisions about the launch? If so, invite only the key decision-makers. Is it to communicate the details to interested parties? If so, then invite anyone who needs to know the details but run the meeting as a briefing group – i.e. presentation and questions rather than a 'free for all'.

Compare the value of the meeting against its costs. Are you likely to get a reasonable return for your investment? Can you achieve your purpose without holding a meeting?

Asking this type of question does a number of things:

- It clarifies for you what you want to get out of the meeting.

- It enables you to communicate that to the people who are attending the meeting so that they can come already tuned in to what is going on.

- It ensures that you invite to your meeting only those people who can make contributions which are directly relevant to the purpose.

Who Should Attend the Meeting

Purposeless gatherings attract large crowds. Convene a meeting to discuss 'management development' and you have created a reason for inviting anyone who may have an interest – personnel, line managers, trainers, car park attendants and so on. Call a meeting to 'review our current use of assessment centres and make recommendations to the board on any changes which are required', and you have a clear purpose which helps to define the 'guest list'. There are a few axioms related to numbers of people at meetings which need repetition here:

- The more people who attend a meeting, the more difficult it is to control.
- Most people attend meetings wanting to speak.
- The length of a contribution increases in inverse proportion to the speaker's understanding of the subject.

If there are people who need to know the results of a meeting but who need not be directly involved in the meeting itself, they can be informed in a number of ways.

- A separate briefing meeting can be arranged with the clear purpose of communicating information. Although this seems like duplication, it is more effective to arrange two meetings with clear purposes than to run one vague rambling meeting.
- Agree to send out minutes promptly to those people who need not attend but who need summaries of decisions taken and actions agreed.
- If someone needs to be present for part of a meeting, then invite them for that part only. If you run your meeting carefully you should be able to say to a contributor 'we will take your presentation at 3 p.m.', thereby saving them time spent waiting to go on and reducing the attendance at your meeting by one.

The Agenda

Let us first clarify what an effective agenda should look like:

- It should explain the purpose of every item for discussion.

- It should clarify any preparatory work that needs to be done before the meeting.

- It should include approximate timings of each agenda item.

- It should be sent out in advance.

By preparing a clear agenda, the chairman helps the participants prepare for the meeting. This enables them to come to the meeting with well-thought out ideas, clear about the contribution they want to make.

The preparation of an agenda ensures that meetings follow a logical order. It is easier to do this in the peace and serenity of your office when writing the agenda than in the hurly-burly of the average business meeting. So even if a meeting is convened to discuss one topic, break that topic down into stages in the agenda to ensure that problems are reviewed before solutions, information is reviewed before recommendations and so on.

Another aspect of ordering the agenda which is often forgotten is that the order of items can help to build up a strong feeling of consensus. The meeting I referred to at the beginning of the chapter ended in conflict. If this happens, the abiding memory of the meeting is the row at the end – hardly an effective way to build a strong team.

Try to start the meeting with a positive, consensus building item. This gets the meeting off to a good start. After this stage, you can introduce any items which are likely to provoke disagreement. These will be approached more positively if consensus has been built at the beginning. Then try to introduce consensus items at the end of the meeting so that the members will leave for home with positive memories of the meeting. This will have two effects:

- It will enhance their commitment to the decisions made at the meeting.

- It will encourage them to come to the next meeting in a positive mood.

The Art of Chairmanship

Chairmanship is a difficult job and a rare skill. Usually the senior person present at a meeting either takes the chair or hijacks it. This is not always a productive idea because the more senior the manager, the more likely he is to make a large contribution. It is difficult enough to run a meeting without adding the burden of trying to react to and comment on everything that is said and done. When the meeting is underway, the chairman is the manager of the meeting. He is there to ensure that the purpose is achieved within the time; and also, that the people attending the meeting have all contributed to that achievement.

There are three responsibilities which the chairman needs to discharge:

Managing the process
Managing the time
Managing the people.

1.   Managing the process

The chairman should understand the purpose of the meeting and have communicated it to the members of the meeting through the agenda. Those two steps are an important precursor to the meeting but the chairman cannot just sit back and expect the meeting to follow the agenda and achieve the purpose which has been set.

The chairman is responsible for making sure that the aims set out in the agenda are achieved. If the discussion shows any signs of wandering off track the chairman must bring it back as smoothly as possible. People digress for a variety of reasons but the effect of digression is the dilution of the original aims and frustration from those people who want to press on and achieve those aims.

The chairman should regularly remind the meeting of the aim of whatever item is under discussion. When there is agreement on a topic, the chairman should be sufficiently assertive to close the discussion. Managers in meetings can be rounded up like sheep but if the shepherd doesn't close the gate of the fold, they can escape along a new path of disagreement or digression.

The easiest way for the chairman to close a topic is to summarize. A well-timed summary leads to a close of the topic and it also clarifies the agreement, whilst providing help for the minute writer.

2.   Managing the time

This is the simplest of the meeting management tasks. All it requires is a good watch and an iron will.

Firstly, the chairman should start the meeting at the published starting time. When a chairman develops a reputation for promptness, people will appear on time. I worked with a works manager who at his first meeting at the factory greeted latecomers with 'eight minutes late', 'ten minutes late'. He didn't need to repeat the performance at the next meeting.

Secondly, time should be allowed to individual agenda items and then adhered to. Timings should be allocated in proportion to the importance of the item. A caveat, however: agenda items cannot be adhered to as closely as start times; there are occasions when a little extra discussion is necessary on a particular item. However, these items should be the exception and not the rule.

Thirdly, the chairman should publish a finishing time and stick to it. Meeting participants are extremely grateful for prompt endings. The effective chairman will ensure that he is aware of items for 'Any Other Business' before the meeting and that time is allowed for them within the agenda.

3.   Managing the people

Meetings are made up not just of minutes, agendas and order papers. They are a group of people who come together to make decisions, solve problems, devise strategies and communicate information. Along with agendas and reports, those people bring with them their personal strengths and weaknesses, prejudices, hobby horses and a whole range of emotional baggage varying from anger to raging paranoia.

The chairman of the meeting has to take all these human frailties into account. There is always an undertow of human relationships within any meeting and the chairman has to take every opportunity to weld the participants together as an effective team.

If there is a strong feeling that conflict is brewing and that major differences of opinion are about to surface, the chairman has to deal with them not by suppression but by encouraging them to come out and be tackled in an open and positive way. The discussion should not end in conflict but a way should be agreed in which the conflict can be resolved.

The chairman also has a responsibility to encourage the reticent group member. It is important to know the team and to be aware of the likely 'shrinking violets'. Silent members need careful watching – silence can be caused by diffidence or hostility. If it is due to hostility it is better to probe it than ignore it. If it is due to diffidence, gentle encouragement will bring out a response.

Finally, it is important to control the waffler. This can usually be done by injecting a sense of briskness into the proceedings which usually discourages loquacity but there are occasions when speakers need to be interrupted. They should be interrupted firmly but politely as they may still have a contribution to make even though they find it difficult to express themselves concisely. Putting people down both alienates them and embarrasses the other members of the team. This can do more damage to the meeting than allowing the long-winded speaker a further five minutes.

The Minutes

Minutes are a record of decisions taken and actions agreed. They are not a blow-by-blow summary of the discussion which took place, unless this is a particular requirement of the circumstances of the meeting. Long minutes have several unwanted effects:

- They are not read by anyone.

- The longer the minutes, the more arguments they are likely to provoke at the next meeting.

- The longer the minutes, the longer they take to be produced and the later they arrive on managers' desks.

Minutes should be concise, easy to read with clear definitions of who is responsible for what. They should consist of un-ambiguous one-liners, so that the recipient can tell at a glance who is responsible for what and when it should be done.

More importantly, they should be written immediately after the meeting or *at* the meeting itself if the chairman summarizes regularly. They should be distributed within 48 hours, so that the meeting participants can act on them while their enthusiasm and commitment is still high. Anyone who distributes minutes of the previous meeting at the next meeting deserves to spend an eternity in boring meetings.

Where to Sit

The effective chairman spends more time on the seating plan than the hostess at a dinner party No, not boy, girl, boy, girl – but using the seating to help the control of the meeting. A few tips:

- Sit the talkative members on your right or left. They will find it more difficult to make eye contact with you and so will find invitations to talk less forthcoming.

- If you anticipate conflict from people, do not sit them opposite each other. Seating is a significant factor in influencing the method of debate. The British parliament with its face-to-face seating is well suited to adversarial politics, whereas the European parliament with its horseshoe is less combative.

- Place a human shield between well known antagonists – do not sit them together or opposite each other.

Self Development Activities

1 Observe carefully any meetings that you attend. Analyse interventions from the chairman, work out why they were made and what effect they had.

2 Practise summarizing discussions that you hear in meetings. Compare your own view with the published minutes.

3 Try to watch the Video Arts film 'Meetings, Bloody Meetings' without blushing.

Afterthought — on Being an Effective Participant

Don't leave it all to the chairman. He may not have read this book.

- Ensure that you do all the preparation that is asked of you. This is the least that you can do.

- Go a stage further and think out where you can make a contribution to the meeting. Go to the meeting with well-thought-out ideas and not half-formed opinions.

- Think where you can't make a contribution and make a

pact with yourself to keep quiet during those times.

- Only speak when you have something to add, don't speak just to reiterate someone else's view and to get your voice heard.

- Allow people to speak. Listen carefully without interruption. Don't spend the intervals between speaking in working out where you can next speak. Listen to other people's contributions.

- If you feel that the meeting is moving away from the point, don't wait for the chairman, try to bring it back on track yourself. But don't use that as a bid for the chairmanship.

- Carry out promptly any actions which you agree to take on.

18
Presenting Your Case in Writing

In any organization, a large proportion of communication must be on paper, otherwise life would be a continual and confusing round of face-to-face meetings and managers would have to rely on their memories far more than they do at present.

Written communication is particularly appropriate under the following circumstances:

- It can be the best method of putting across a complicated subject or argument as it enables the reader to learn at their own pace.

- It is an effective way of capturing an agreement in print. Minutes of meetings and contracts are kept in writing not necessarily out of lack of trust but out of the need for the parties concerned to have an unambiguous reference document and for people not present at the discussion to be able to see what was agreed.

- It is a cheap and reliable way to reach a mass audience and to ensure that they all receive the same message.

- It is the most effective way of transmitting statistics accurately.

However, written communication is not always the best medium.

- It is impersonal and does not have the same impact as other media. It cannot motivate or arouse people as effectively as television, film, radio or the spoken voice. The advent of totalitarianism was brought about partly by replacing print with other media. Print is cold and logical and often unobtrusive.

- Some people find it difficult to learn by reading. The language of written communication is more formal and less colloquial than spoken English.

- It is hard to develop skills by reading about them; although reading is a very helpful method in conjunction with other media, to reinforce skills which have been learned.

- Written communication does not make it easy for the reader to clarify understanding by asking questions. If the recipients of a memo or report do not understand it they will either ignore it or carry out what they understand it to mean. They are unlikely to ring the writer up and ask for clarification.

- Ineffective managers hide behind the written word to avoid confrontation – poisoned memo writers are the bane of any organization.

- There are very few people who can write clear, unambiguous prose. It is therefore very easy to ignore written communications because of boredom or confusion. You can tear up a memo, or put a report in the wastepaper bin. The writer can never be completely sure that the reader has read a report or letter.

The first lesson in written communication is to think through what you want to say and then decide on the most appropriate medium. Only put pen to paper if you are sure it is the best medium for your particular message.

Training in written communication is particularly important. A systematic approach to writing saves the writer time in preparing and writing; it also saves the valuable reading time of the readers as well as avoiding costly misunderstandings.

First — Learn your ABC

Some people find writing easy; some sweat buckets over writing reports or memos. The good news is that everyone can learn to write effectively. There are many books which deal with writing clear prose and anyone who writes regularly for the consumption of other managers should read a book like *The Complete Plain Words* (see bibliography).

A well known mnemonic for communicators is ABC – Accuracy, Brevity, Clarity. These three words should be remembered by any writer:

A = Accuracy. Ensure that the content of your work is based on fact and not guesswork. Also, use words to convey exactly the right meaning.

B = Brevity. The more brief and concise your work, the quicker you will write it and the quicker your reader will both read and understand it.

C = Clarity. Make sure that your meaning is clear and unambiguous. Avoid using a clever allusion if it will distort the clarity of your writing.

The style that you adopt in your writing should always be consistent with these principles. In addition, you need to consider your reader; what is their technical knowledge, their education, their vocabulary? Once you have considered this you can aim your writing much more specifically at your target audience. Writers should remember that they may not be around when the reader picks up the report or letter, so they cannot be asked to clarify any confusing statements.

All written communications are made up of words, sentences, paragraphs and punctuation. The skill is using the right ones in the right way.

1 Words – Too many long words in a piece of writing make it cumbersome and difficult to follow. They also reduce the target audience; the more abstract the words, the better educated your reader needs to be. The purpose of business writing is to communicate and not to impress your reader with the size of your vocabulary; you should write using words which can be understood clearly.

2 Sentences – If words are shorter, sentences are also likely to be shorter; although the writer still needs to be ruthless in cutting down the length of sentences. They should not contain too many subordinate clauses and should express one major idea. Sentences should not be of the same length throughout a piece of work, otherwise it becomes monotonous.

3 Paragraphs – Paragraphs have two functions. They break up a page of written work so that it is easier on the reader's eye. More important, however, is that they break up the content of the written work into separate units of thought. A paragraph should contain only unified ideas and concepts and a writer who wishes to move the discussion on to a new subject or a new facet of a subject should start a new paragraph.

4 *Punctuation* – Grammarians have written whole books about punctuation and have generally failed to agree on such abstruse topics as the correct use of the colon. Punctuation is, however, like bars and rests in music, a way of helping the reader to separate the thoughts of the writer. The writer should read his own work out loud and see if the punctuation clarifies it or makes it less clear.

5 *Jargon* – Jargon is a professional language, clear only to the initiated. It should only be used between fellow professionals who speak the same language and never in communications to the uninitiated.

Report Writing

Reports are written for a variety of reasons: to give information; to make recommendations; to convey ideas and so on. Whatever their purpose, all reports should be written to present facts and opinions in a systematic way. Learning to write reports effectively is an important managerial skill. Approaching a report systematically enables the manager to save time in producing it; it is written in a way which enables the receiver of the report to extract the information he needs as quickly as possible and because of this the author is more likely to achieve his objectives. There are five stages involved in the writing of a report:

Aims
Information gathering
Arrangement
Writing
Revision

1 *Aims.* The report writer needs to clarify the following:
Why am I writing this report?
In what form is it required?
Who will be my primary reader?
Who else will see copies?

At what level of detail should I write?
What am I trying to achieve?

2 Information gathering. The approach to this stage varies
with the technical requirements of the subject of the report.
Commonsense tells us that information is broken into three
categories:

Known/Relevant – This category of information needs little
investigation, although we need to examine it critically to
ensure that we have made no assumptions.

Known/Irrelevant – Resist the temptation to include in your
report information which is not relevant. You will not impress
people with the breadth of your knowledge, you will merely
irritate them.

Unknown/Relevant – This area demands investigation. We
can assess relevance by asking, 'What information would the
reader want on this?'.

3 Arrangement. Putting a report in a logical order helps
both the writer and the reader. The discipline of writing
systematically helps the writer to put thoughts in order. Seeing
a report set out in a logical order helps the reader to work
quickly. A good report should anticipate the questions that a
reader will ask in the order that they will ask them. Typically
these will be as follows:

Reader's questions	How the writer anticipates
'Is this report worth reading?'	A synopsis at the beginning of the report. A synopsis is a summary of the major points of a report and should include: The aims of the report. The main points. Alternative courses of action. Recommendations.

Reader's questions	How the writer anticipates
'What was the writer trying to achieve?'	After the synopsis, the writer should set out the introduction to include: A detailed statement of aims. The terms of reference. The method of investigation and a number of administrative points such as: Date. Distribution list. Classifications of confidentiality.
'What are the facts?'	The main body of the report is made up initially of facts and interpretations as follows: Facts obtained (state source). Analysis of facts. Interpretation of facts. The statement of facts should be as concise as possible; only those facts which are relevant to the aims should be included.
'OK, so what can we do about it?'	Finish off the main body of the report by setting out the options available to the reader.

Reader's questions	*How the writer anticipates*
'But what do you propose we do about it?'	The report should end, naturally enough, with recommendations and conclusions. These should be concise and lead on logically from the analysis of facts in the main body of the report. The conclusions and recommendations should be in more detail than those set out in the synopsis.
'I'd like a little more information. Have you got some of the statistics that you based your recommendations on?'	Some managers like to read a short concise report; others like to wallow in facts and statistics. Write the report for the former but if you work for a 'statistics buff' attach them to the report as an appendix. The non-technical people will not have to wade through the detail; the nit-picker can grasp the main points before picking his nits.

4   *Writing.* When you are writing a report, don't take small pockets of time or try to write a large report in one chunk. An ideal time is between one and two hours. Much less than an hour isn't enough to get into the work; few people can concentrate hard for more than two hours without losing effectiveness.

5   *Revision.* Read your draft as if you were the intended recipient. Do this after a day or so if possible. Is it clear? Are there any ambiguities? Is your case watertight? Get a friend to read it – not always a very good friend, they may be reluctant to be critical.

When your work is typed, don't rely on the typist to proof-read. Check if there is a house-style and stick to it; don't run the risk of the recipient being distracted from the content by errors in presentation.

Some other points about presentation:

6   *Presenting statistics.* Make use of visual presentations when presenting accounts, statistical summaries or costings. For example, pie charts are simple and clear; they are useful for presenting technical or financial information to laymen, showing how component parts make up the whole. Graphs and bar charts are equally clear and concise ways of presenting figures.

7   *Numbering sections.* Number your report in a decimal sequence. I find it preferable to the variety of systems which many reports use. See Figure 2.

Figure 2

1.   Main purpose of report.
     1.1   Summarize the main arguments in the current union dispute.
     1.2   Recommend a course of action for the next meeting with the Divisional Officer.

2.   Information.
     2.1   Wage costs during 1984/5
           2.1.1.   Normal costs
           2.1.2.   Overtime costs
           2.1.3.   Welfare payments

and so on.

A decimal system is clear for reference purposes and can be more clearly referred to over the telephone.

Writing a Good Letter

Dear Reader,

Writing an effective business letter

We have already discussed some of the principles of good writing and also the correct way to plan and structure a report. Many of these principles apply when writing business letters.

Letter writing is an important part of business life. Well written letters make the task of both writer and reader easier;

they can also enhance or detract from the reputation of both the writer and the company they represent.

Business letters should be written systematically, following a simple structure:

Introduction – State the purpose of the letter and the event which prompted you to write.

Facts – Set out the facts clearly and in a logical order.

Action – Clarify what action is required and who is responsible for taking it.

Concluding remarks – It is customary to conclude a letter with a polite statement.

As well as following this structure, business letters should be written in direct, clear language. Writers of old-fashioned commercial English used to pad out letters with such useless phrases as 'We are in receipt of' and 'Thank you for your esteemed enquiry' – these should be avoided. Otherwise, follow the advice given in previous sections of this chapter.

I hope this information will be useful to you.

Yours faithfully,

The author.

The Manager as Dictator
or dictating to a secretary and audio dictation

Dictation is a useful skill to learn but many managers find it difficult. It is worth persevering with as it has great potential for saving time. There are two main methods:

- *Dictating to a secretary* – There are few things more daunting than seeing a secretary poised with pen and shorthand pad, waiting for you to dictate. Experienced and articulate managers dry up with fear. Avoid dictator's 'dry-up' by pre-planning the letter, also give the secretary all the relevant papers. Dictate in phrases if possible. If you do dry up or slow down, send your secretary out to allow you to do more thinking and to allow the secretary to get on with other work.

- *Audio Dictation* – Pre-plan your dictation and remember that the typist cannot always ask you for clarification. Check that the tape is recording and give the typist instructions about the number of copies needed, any layout problems and headings. Don't leave instructions to the end of the tape; secretaries have been known to burst into tears upon hearing at the end of the tape – 'two carbon copies, please'. Give punctuation as you go along and check that the paragraphs are flagged. Spell difficult names. A final point – if you make a mistake, don't utter an audible obscenity, mouth it silently to yourself and rewind the tape.

Handling Incoming Paperwork

Receiving written communication consists of three stages: reading, note taking and action.

Reading. Effective reading consists of two important skills: deciding what to read and reading those things quickly.

Firstly, it is necessary to sift through the mass of reading material available to the manager and decide what needs to be read. Put a priority on those items to clarify whether they need to be read immediately or can be shelved until a convenient time. If you are on a circulation list and you aren't ready to read the article, then put 'later' against your name and pass it on to someone for whom it may have more immediate relevance.

Those things that you need to read should then be read more effectively. Learn to scan articles for relevant facts rather than reading everything at the same pace. Adapt your reading speed to the requirement of the written work you are studying; interesting but non-essential articles should be scanned, technical manuals need to be read and digested slowly.

Note taking. An important part of receiving both verbal and written communication is retaining what you have discovered. This retention is vastly improved by taking short notes on *key* ideas and concepts. I stress the word 'key' because the majority of words that we hear are not necessary for retention purposes. Our memory is more sophisticated than we realize and usually it only needs a key word to trigger off a chain of recollection.

Action. Paperwork is one of the areas which managers detest. The effective manager tries to reduce the amount of paper handled by dealing with it as quickly as possible.

In order to achieve these objectives follow the following rules:

- Ask only for information you need and can use, otherwise you waste hours of your time and everybody else's.

- Encourage your staff to practise 'exception reporting', whereby they give you reports only on situations outside the norm; not on every detail of every activity.

- Paper that you don't need should be filed under WPB – waste paper basket. Only retain paper that you genuinely need.

- Encourage your secretary to weed out unnecessary paper.

- Keep a clear desk. Using your desk as a large, flat pending tray ensures that you don't forget things and that is usually the problem. Too many stacked piles of tomorrow's paperwork are distracting.

- Develop a paperflow system – IN, PENDING and OUT.

- Don't pick up a piece of paper without taking some action on it.

Self Development Activities

1 Read regularly. Journalists in particular develop a concise writing style – they have to write interesting and accurate work within tight deadlines.

2 Read actively. Analyse good written work – ask why is it effective. Then do likewise – without losing your own natural style.

3 Keep a notebook of useful words and phrases. Plagiarize other people's written work.

4 Try to go on a speedreading course, especially if your work involves you in a lot of reading.

19
Negotiating

We all negotiate every day in business. We negotiate often in our family and private lives. We cannot help bargaining and so it is important to consider how to get the most out of our negotiations.

Apart from formal commercial or industrial relations negotiations, there are a wide range of events in which we find ourselves negotiating:

- With the finance director in the run-up to the annual budget.

- Pressing for a salary rise.

- Persuading our staff to stay late to handle a particularly urgent problem.

- Agreeing the time at which our children should come home from a party.

- Making amends to our spouse when we are likely to be late home on our wedding anniversary.

Negotiating is the technique of bargaining in which two parties attempt to reach a mutually acceptable agreement. This is an important definition. As you can see, it makes no reference to winning or losing. That is because the concept of 'winning' in negotiations is different from any other walk of life. Winning a negotiation is only possible if both sides accept the final agreement. If one side has used its current strong bargaining position to force a solution on the other party, then although it may have won a battle, there is no doubt that it has created a future adversary and may well be under pressure when the balance of power tilts the other way.

An example of this from international relations is the Treaty of Versailles. Viewed at the time, the allies could be said to have 'won' the negotiation but only at the cost of creating conditions in Germany which led to the rise of Hitler and ultimately to the Second World War.

Of course, it is unlikely that any of your negotiations will cause a Third World War but the seeds of crisis and dispute are sown in apparently victorious negotiations.

Negotiations are not exercises in chess-playing logic. They are carried out between people and thus are fraught with emotion and prejudice. The nature of negotiation creates great potential for conflict and many gambits in negotiation are aimed at the person and not the problem. You should avoid these techniques but you must expect that the other party may not. The important thing to remember is *don't take anything personally.* When you do, you lose your objectivity and you reveal to your opponent your areas of vulnerability.

Research and common sense tell us a number of things about negotiation:

- People with high aspirations are likely to achieve more than people with low aspirations.

- Negotiators with clear objectives and a well considered strategy are more likely to succeed than the negotiator who plays it by ear.

- The longer you listen carefully to your opponent, the more likely you are to understand their objectives.

- Never give anything away, always trade it.

- Constructive argument is always better than vulgar abuse.

I am always concerned when I hear one of the following phrases before a negotiation:

'I'm just going to go in and listen to what they have to say.'
'Let's play this one by ear.'
'I just want to get as much as I can from them.'
'I'm pretty flexible about this one.'

Preparation is the key to successful negotiation. The negotiator who fails to clarify his aims or to prepare his strategy will always be vulnerable to an opponent who has done these things. Without preparation and careful planning, you can only react to your opponent's aims and without anticipating those you will find it difficult to put forward clear arguments to resist them.

We hear a lot in politics about trying to win the middle ground. Negotiation is a similar process. Both sides start out by putting forward their 'best' position. This is the most optimistic result for them; like an army pitching camp on a hill, hoping that the opponents will come to them and fight the battle on their ground. When both sides have declared their position, it is then a matter of bargaining to arrive at an agreement near to your best position. A trade union official once said of wage negotiations with the board of a national-ized industry, 'We are moving towards an agreement, natur-ally I expect the board to move more quickly than we will.'

Both sides also have a 'break-off' position. This marks the limit of their movement away from their best position and is located at a point where the parties would prefer to end the negotiations rather than settle beyond that point.

Figure 3

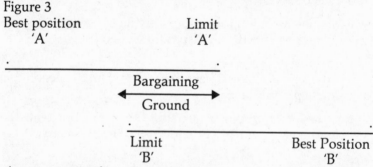

As you can see from Figure 3, the bargaining ground is likely to be the overlap of the two lines between the limits that both sides set themselves. The limit may be based on price, budget, principle or the level of authority of the negotiator.

If the two lines do not overlap and the limit positions of both sides are mutually unacceptable, then this is known as 'deadlock' and one or both parties have to persuade the other to move their position.

Between the limit and the best position, the effective negotiator leaves a milestone which is called a 'fall-back position'. If a fall-back position is not clarified, the negotiator can move too quickly from best position to limit.

Good preparation must clarify the following:

- Your own 'best position'
- Your own 'break-off position'
- Your own 'fall-back position'
- Your opponent's 'best position'
- Your opponent's 'break-off' position

Clarifying your own Position

The diagram representing the negotiating positions is of course a great simplification of what is usually a very complex process. There is rarely one position and that position is rarely static. Negotiations almost always involve a range of connected issues, some of which are important and necessary conditions for a settlement, others being things which are less important and can be traded off for something else. It is essential that the negotiator has a clear view of his interests and aims before going into the bargaining room. What are those important aims which must be met if the negotiations are to be successful? If they are not clarified then there is a danger that they may be discarded in a fit of absentmindedness. What are the limits of your negotiating position? At what stage do you stop negotiating? If they ask for a lower price for your product, are there other factors that you can adjust without going beyond your limit?

These questions must be answered. Otherwise you will achieve your opponent's objective without achieving your own and that is the worst of all possible worlds.

Understanding your Opponent's Position

Once you have clarified your position, it is important to consider your opponent and what he is likely to want from the negotiation. Firstly, what is your opponent like? Have you met him before? Does he set high targets and retreat quickly, or does he have modest aspirations and stick to them?

Secondly, what are the most and the least that he is likely to want out of these negotiations? Gathering intelligence is an important part of negotiations. It covers thinking about your opponent's position, his aspirations, his declared policy and his public statements.

If you were an American negotiator in an arms control meeting, what would you want to know? The size and quality of Russian missiles, their deployment and the likely targets? To find the Russian 'best position' you would read *Pravda*. To understand Russian negotiating behaviour you would study past conferences and read Lenin. There would be a wealth of information available to you. In the same way, dealing with customers and trades unions, there is a tremendous amount of information – policy statements, conference speeches, annual reports, past negotiating behaviour, agreements made with competitors and so on. Time spent in reconnaissance is seldom wasted and you should do your homework thoroughly before a negotiation.

Strategy

Having clarified the likely positions which you and your opponent will take, you now have to consider how you will come to a mutually agreeable solution. You need to work out a strategy. The strategy must be flexible because your opponent will probably not wish to fit in with it and thus it must take account of contingencies which may arise during the negotiations.

In a short chapter it is impossible to cover all the strategic options. There are, however, a number of factors which you should keep in mind.

- Don't take stances. Remember to negotiate to achieve your aims, not to win a particular debating point. The history of British industrial relations is littered with strikes which contributed nothing to the interests of the union members; those have been sacrificed to protect an entrenched position of a union official. This behaviour is like the generals in the First World War attacking a hill which had no strategic importance purely to claim a victory. There is no money to be exchanged for debating points in a negotiation; concentrate on achieving your aims.

- In any negotiation with a customer, supplier, trade

union, finance director, wife or child, you gain nothing by an approach which damages the relationship. Even in the most vitriolic industrial dispute, the parties have to work together again one day. If the relationship has broken down then negotiations become impossible. In almost every case it is wise to move a little way to prevent a relationship breaking down.

- Keep a range of alternatives in mind. If the issues are complex then there are many more avenues to explore. Explore them all, especially don't be tied down by precedent. In a commercial negotiation keep price, quantity, quality, delivery dates and so on in your mind; don't just haggle over price.

- Concentrate on solutions which increase the size of the cake rather than those which are only concerned with who gets the biggest piece. If a company and union are negotiating a productivity deal they should be trying to make that deal really effective so that it increases sales and profits as well as the income of the employees. Too often the debate becomes hung up on the 'no bonus without increase; no increase without a bonus' circular argument. If both sides have clear aims they should be able to collaborate on developing solutions which enable both sides to achieve those aims.

Team Roles

If the negotiation is carried out by a team, it is essential that the approach is clarified. Who acts as proposer? Who requests adjournments? When can members of the team speak? Discipline in negotiation is very important. Any inconsistencies between team members will be picked up by the opposition and can be used to split off members of the negotiating team from each other.

Into the Bargaining Arena

Preparation is important in a negotiation but even the best prepared negotiator needs to adhere to some sensible behavioural guidelines in the negotiation. Negotiation is a matter of bargaining with each side trying to achieve their objectives. In a negotiation there are a number of activities; they do not always follow a strict sequence but they can be observed in most negotiations, as follows:

- The presentation of a case

- Listening to a presentation

- Argument

- Bargaining

- Agreement.

Presenting

Both sides begin by presenting their case. At this stage, you should be stating your best case very clearly. You are staking out your position and making clear what is the most that you want to get out of the negotiation. There is no excuse for not presenting this effectively as it is the only part of the negotiation that you can prepare almost verbatim. There are three main rules here.

- Present your case *positively*. Start off by showing that you are well-briefed and confident. A nervous, apologetic opening will start to push you downhill and will give your opponent a great boost.

- Present your case *precisely*. Use words accurately and try not to blur the edges of the negotiation by accident. It is, of course, permissible to use a deliberately vague expression to signal your willingness to move on a particular point but by using words imprecisely you may make a signal that you were not intending to make.

- Be *polite*. Avoid emotive language, sly digs at your opponent, vulgar abuse and bad manners. If your opponent uses these as tactics, resist them firmly and do not lose your temper. An angry negotiator is a potential loser. However, controlled anger is a useful ploy if it is planned. Remember Kruschev's shoe banging ploy in the United Nations? There was photographic evidence that while he was banging his shoe in the United

Nations, he was actually wearing shoes on both feet. The shoe had been smuggled in by an aide! It is equally true that Macmillan asked 'Can we have a translation of that?', showing that a temper tantrum need not always terrorize the opposition.

Listening

Listen very carefully to your opponent. Listen actively; this is your opportunity to understand his case and to weigh up his best position. Take notes or make sure that one of your team is taking notes. Some important points:

- After you have listened, ask questions. Clarify any points that you don't understand. Use the time to develop a clear understanding of your opponent's case. Don't stop questioning until you are aware of the complete shopping list.

- Listen for signals. If your opponent uses words carefully he will signify very subtly where concessions are likely to be made. In particular, qualified statements signal possible ground for bargaining. For example, 'My committee will not let me discuss productivity payments at this stage' means 'If you give me concessions in other areas, I may be able to persuade them to discuss productivity later.'

Arguing

Arguing is the stage when the basis of the case is examined and analysed. There are a number of important skills to be learned here, the stage before the bargaining really starts. If I may use a boxing analogy, this is the time for 'bobbing and weaving': testing your opponent's defences by a few well aimed jabs, keeping your defences up to avoid his jabbing. Argument skills such as the following are as important as arguing your own points clearly and logically.

- *Questioning.* Asking open questions which your opponent must answer is an effective way of understanding your opponent's arguments.

- *Summarizing.* Playing back to your opponent your understanding of his case and the state of the negotiations so far is an effective way of breaking deadlock and clarifying misunderstanding.

- *Adjourning.* If the arguing phase becomes vitriolic or the negotiation is taking an unexpected turn, try to adjourn and take a think break.

Bargaining

Bargaining is the crucial part of the negotiation. You should by now be fully aware of the limits of your opponent's case. The issues should be particularly clear and it is now appropriate to move towards bargaining and thus towards a solution.

Bargaining is the process of exchanging and trading things which you have for things that you want. In wage negotiations, the company has access to cash, the union has control over a quantity of labour. Both parties want part of what the other side have but they need to give up something of their own to get it. How much they need to give up depends on two things:

- Their bargaining position
- Their bargaining skill.

These two factors cannot be judged in isolation. People in a poor bargaining position can extract large concessions from a more powerful opponent if they display effective bargaining skills.

The bargaining position was once succinctly described by a union official in the motor industry – 'When you want cars, we screw you. When you have enough cars, you screw us.' It is far more subtle than that in most negotiations but cannot be explained more effectively. Each side has to analyse their bargaining position in relation to the opposition and to perceive each side's strengths and weaknesses. This perception is important – it will not help to be in a strong position if you do not recognize and exploit it. Students of history will view Chamberlain's ill-fated negotiations with Hitler as an example of this. The League of Nations' powers were far stronger than Hitler's Germany at the time of Munich and yet they did not use this advantage in their negotiations. Instead, they allowed him time to build up his strength.

Bargaining skills are very important in order to make the best use of the negotiating position.

- Never give anything away, always trade it away in return for something else, e.g. 'If you agree to an earlier delivery date, we will reinstate the five per cent over-rider.' The statement of an offer must always be conditional on a reciprocal concession. The 'IF' is a qualification in the contract which allows you to withdraw the offer if the qualification is not met.

- Keep the whole of your package and theirs in mind at all times. This will enable you to select the areas in which you are prepared to make concessions and those areas in which you want your opponent to make concessions.

Agreement

The experienced negotiator knows that the longer a negotiation goes on the more time is available to both extract and make concessions. The closure of a negotiation becomes a matter of judgement. If you are starting to feel pressure it may be in your interests to close and withdraw, but if you feel that you are likely to gain more you will naturally want to keep going longer. Whatever the timing of the close, both sides must close either by agreement or by sanctions which take the matter out of the negotiating arena. The latter is an unwelcome step but sometimes preferable to making un-necessary concessions. The first option – agreement – by definition involves both sides in an acceptable solution which they can both agree. Thus the closing position or final offer must be:

- *Credible.* Don't make final offers if they are not final. Your opponent will test this and if you start to concede that position will push you even further.

- *Acceptable.* Your final offer must take into account your opponent's aims. If not, they are unlikely to agree and more likely to break off negotiations or accept grudgingly because of their poor negotiating position. If they do this, they will wait for an appropriate time to 'screw you' and you may have won this negotiation at the expense of the next one.

When you have agreed, capture that agreement in print and make sure that the terms of the agreement are crystal clear. If the agreement is oral then send a written summary to your opponent very quickly after the negotiation.

Self Development Activities

1 Try to observe negotiations before taking an active part in any yourself. Acting as 'recording angel' can be very helpful to the negotiating team and yourself.

2 Listen to current affairs programmes on industrial disputes. Estimate the 'best' position and 'limit' positions of each party.

20
Managing a Crisis

One of the important principles in negotiation is trying to maintain the relationship between the two parties. Unions and management, buyers and suppliers, directors and their colleagues, husbands and wives all have to work together when the negotiation is over. However, sometimes in negotiations relationships undergo a period of 'crisis' – that is a period when the relationship reaches a turning point and is particularly vulnerable. If the relationship is to survive then the crisis must be managed.

There have been many studies in international relations of the management of crisis. In the international context, a crisis is potentially cataclysmic and so it needs to be managed and controlled in precisely the right way. Take the Cuban missile crisis. If President Kennedy had been 'softer', then the Soviet Union would have enjoyed a significant advantage in the balance of power with missiles in the heart of the American sphere of influence. If he had been 'harder', then the world may well have been at war with appalling consequences.

A crisis can be between two adversaries or two colleagues; both types of crisis need to be managed in the same way. You may have a dispute with your suppliers or two departments in the same company can be battling it out against one another. Both situations are harmful to your business if they are not resolved.

Decision-making can be difficult in a crisis; when raw emotions are bared and people are in dispute there is a tendency to make rash emotional decisions which exacerbate rather than ameliorate the problem. A crisis slide can then occur when everyone is dragged into a vortex of argument and vulgar abuse.

There are a number of rules which help to keep the relationship going during a crisis. It is important to hit the right approach – managing a crisis is neither destroying your opponents nor capitulating to them.

1   *Use minimum sanctions first.* It is easier to move up the scale of force than to move down it. You want to exert yourself as little as possible initially so that you can achieve your aims by the most effective method. Taking a sledgehammer to crack a nut is only a productive policy when you have tried to see whether the nutcrackers will work. You should be prepared to move up the scale if the first approach doesn't work.

2   *Decide how far you will go.* A crisis slide takes place when people fail to put limits on the sanctions that they are prepared to use in a given situation. Both parties keep responding to each other's aggression until one side takes some action which goes just one step further than they really want to take. An effective crisis manager is very clear about the level of response which he is prepared to make and always keeps his interests in mind. Cutting off your nose to spite your face is far too common in many commercial or industrial crises – a strike which costs union members more than they stand to gain in the wage negotiations; breaking relationships with a supplier of high quality goods because of a contractual dispute – both of these are examples of a dispute going further than it needed.

3   *Keep the future in mind.* Every action that you take is the baseline for the future. Do not do anything that you feel sets an unhappy precedent for the future. Also, remember that in most cases you will have to work with your 'opponent' when the crisis is over. This is particularly important in an intra-mural crisis between departments. Before you abuse the accountant in the ritual pre-budget bloodshed, remember that he will be monitoring your department's performance for the remainder of the financial year.

4   *Keep your options open.* Keep a wide range of options available and try not to narrow those options yourself or allow them to be reduced by your opponent. Avoid going down a track which inevitably leads to confrontation unless you are absolutely sure that you are prepared to suffer both the confrontation and its short- and long-term consequences.

5   *Don't hem your opponent in.* Always try to give your opponent an option other than confrontation. Allow him to retreat without losing face. The macho manager enjoys push-

ing people into a confrontation but two things can happen –
either the opponent apparently retreats with his lost face and
stores up bile for another confrontation (remember the Treaty
of Versailles) or he turns and fights like a cornered animal and
so the crisis becomes more costly and damaging to both sides.

6 *Keep your lines of communication intact.* Even if you
are in the middle of a crisis with your opponent, never break
off communication. While channels of communication are
open there is a chance of a constructive solution to the crisis. In
international affairs the recall of an ambassador is a serious
step because it breaks the line of communication. If you don't
want to talk directly to your opponent, use an intermediary
but make sure that your intentions are communicated clearly
by someone you can trust. In Britain during the last few years
we have seen the growing importance of ACAS in industrial
disputes. All mediators believe that while talking, even
indirectly, is going on then the crisis is still being managed.

7 *Make sure that your case is well publicized.* If your
dispute is likely to become public – an industrial dispute, a
commercial dispute or an inter-departmental disagreement,
make sure that as many people as possible understand your
case. Many industrial disputes are lost in the public arena and
it is important to clarify your case rather than be seen always
to be responding to your opponent's case.

Remember, manage a crisis, don't react to it.

Self Development Activities

1 Read anything you can about the Cuban missile crisis. It is
a golden example of crisis management.
2 Study political and industrial crises. Analyse them
carefully and watch out for those features which move them
towards a solution.

21
Improving Staff Performance — Motivation

A lot has been written about motivation but not a lot of it has been read, at least not by the people who are responsible for motivating others. The Home for Bewildered Managers has a library full of books and courses about motivation which have been used by trainers and consultants over the years. In general they amount to a pinch of Maslow, some MacGregor and a huge dollop of Herzberg. Managers rarely want to read the original text, they want to know in practical terms how they can get the best out of their staff.

This chapter and the next two are about improving staff performance. The three areas are very closely linked and are related to a very simple model.

Everybody has a range of performance within which they carry out their work. The range varies from an upper limit dictated by ability (intellectual or physical) and zero performance, which is the lower limit. Within that range is a level of acceptability which is the lowest standard of work that the boss will tolerate without taking disciplinary action. Thus the range of performance for each individual looks like this.

Figure 4

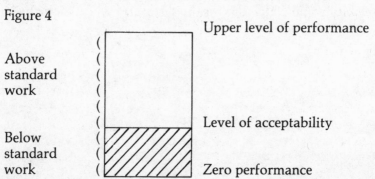

Upper level of performance

Above standard work

Level of acceptability

Below standard work

Zero performance

The manager's responsibility for the performance of staff can thus be summarized in three main functions:

- Motivating staff to perform at the upper limit of performance.

- Coaching staff so that they develop their ability and thus increase their potential for high quality work. (See chapter 22.)

- Clarifying and enforcing the level of acceptability so that poor performers are given the opportunity to discuss and evaluate their performance. (See chapter 23.)

It is important to understand these as separate functions. Motivation can only improve performance so far; then it becomes a matter of developing new or additional skills. An athletics coach cannot make an Olympic sprinter out of a seedy, overweight novice purely by motivation. He will have to teach sprinting techniques and use training programmes to develop particular muscles, to improve lung function and so on.

The main theories of motivation focus on both the 'inner man' and the environment in which man works. Herzberg's theory, for example, takes the view that environmental factors alone cannot motivate but that their absence can demotivate. Positive motivation, in his view, comes from within the individual and the effective manager understands this and builds on the intrinsic satisfaction which human beings naturally gain from working.

I shall take it as read that human beings enjoy work and find it as natural as any other activity. Managers and directors actually put barriers in their way more often than they encourage people to work. The following are my suggestions for ten ways to improve your staff's performance.

1 *Set clear and unambiguous standards.* A blinding glimpse of the obvious is that people work better when they know what is expected of them. I have said this on countless training courses and been told that 'everyone knows that'. Of course they do and yet there are many people who still do not know precisely what their boss expects of them and, even more worrying, there are bosses who are not able to tell you precisely what they expect of their staff. From the first day of

the induction course, every manager should explain to every member of their staff what is expected of them, what standards they are expected to achieve and what targets they have been set.

2   *Tell people how they are doing.* The people who work for you are not idiots. If you tell them the standard you expect and then give them regular reports on how they match up to those standards, they will work out for themselves how they can improve. How are you assessed? By sales, stocks, production quotas, costs, labour turnover and so on. As a manager are you told how you are performing in relation to budget? If you are, then you will probably not need to be told where to make improvements if you fall below budget.

3   *Thank people for good work.* Now this is really revolutionary. 'Thank you' is a simple phrase which implies both recognition and gratitude for work carried out. It has to be sincere and should not be given in lieu of a pay rise, otherwise it is being used for manipulation rather than motivation.

4   *Point out and criticize poor work.* Although I am dealing with the poor performer a couple of chapters on, nevertheless poor work needs to be considered here too. Even the best worker can produce some poor work and it is important that below standard work is pointed out and corrected. Otherwise the good worker may start to lapse if he knows that any work of poor standard will slip through the net. The important thing in correcting poor performance is to criticize the work and not the worker. Saying to a member of staff 'That was a poor report. It was not up to your usual standard' is a criticism of the piece of work which does not attack or threaten the worker. By contrast, saying 'You idiot, that report was typical of you – short on facts and badly presented' is an attack on the worker which will make him feel humiliated. The first example is corrective, the second will leave the member of staff smarting after your attack on him rather than on the poor report he has presented. An effective reprimand is:

- Short and sharp
- Carried out in private

- Aimed at correcting the performance not insulting the performer

- Ended on a positive note

5 *Treat people as individuals.* Everyone has a different psychological make up. Their needs differ and an effective manager recognizes this and adjusts his manner to the individual. Some people are timid and shy, they need to be brought out and given a gentle boost to their confidence. More robust people would resent that kind of treatment. Get to know your staff and find out what motivates them and then use that as the basis of your approach to them.

6 *Give people responsibility.* The men and women who work for us have families and mortgages, run a house and a car, act as secretaries of local organizations – in short, they are responsible people. They come to work and we treat them like children, and potentially delinquent children at that. People can take more responsibility than we think. The only reason that they do not is that organizations have demoralized them over the years and convinced them that they are unable to handle responsibility. Treating people as adults is an important step in managing them correctly. Treat them like children and they will act like children.

7 *Put the job in context.* Explain why you are asking your staff to do a particular job. They will be more interested in it and more likely to perform with enthusiasm if they see an end result. Division of labour has pushed us into specialized jobs in which we are unable to see the whole job performed. Take your staff to see the product of their labours – the customer, the finished machine, the suppliers and so on.

8 *Provide the right working environment.* If ever you hear of a director refusing to spend money on staff facilities or on decorating the workplace, go and look into his office. You will probably see a large desk, carpet two inches thick, paintings on the wall, a coffee table and two easy chairs. We all work better in a pleasant, light environment and money spent on refurbishing is rarely wasted. Lavishness is not necessary but a depressing environment tells employees what the company thinks about them and their welfare.

9 *Be approachable.* Try to be visible and approachable to your staff – they may need your guidance. It is important to have someone to share problems with and people perform well

if they know that the manager is available to help and give advice.

10 *Pay good money.* The motivating effect of pay and rations is one of the regular sidelines in the motivation debate. The consensus view is that extra money does not improve performance in the long term although it might in the short term. What is certain, however, is that low pay does have a detrimental effect on performance. This is all common sense. You may enjoy your work but if you know that you are underpaid you feel a strong sense of grievance which must ultimately have an effect on the way you work. You are given a pay rise and, in the short term, your gratitude boosts your performance. That new level of pay soon becomes the norm and so the incentive effect falls off and other motivators take effect. In summary, paying your staff well does not necessarily motivate but paying them badly actively demotivates.

Self Development Activities

1 Write down the names of all your staff. Write against each one what you feel motivates them.

2 Look for opportunities to recognize good work.

3 Do read Maslow, Herzberg and MacGregor if the opportunity arises. They do give some useful insights into behaviour at work.

22
Improving Staff Performance
— Coaching and Delegation

When children learn, they do not usually attend training courses or read manuals on tying shoe laces or using crayons. They learn by doing things, getting them wrong and then reviewing that experience with their parents. My daughter has learned not to touch the dog when the dog is eating. She learned this by doing it once, the dog snarled at her and I explained 'little girls shouldn't touch doggies when they are eating'. This simple but effective method of learning continues throughout our lives. When we become managers we call it 'coaching'.

Coaching is a way of helping someone to learn. It is different from teaching or training because a good coach spends much more time listening and questioning than lecturing and explaining. There are three basic ideas which underpin coaching:

Active learning. Everyone will tell you that you only learn by experience. This is very true but only if you take the trouble to review that experience and extract lessons from it. People who never do anything will never learn anything but in order to learn effectively those who do things must review them carefully, preferably with someone (a coach) who is experienced and skilled in helping them to draw conclusions from their experience.

The boss. As the child learns from the parent, so the employee learns from their boss. The boss sets performance standards, conducts appraisals, reviews results and sets priorities; naturally this will have a great impact on the staff's performance. This learning will be carried out whether the boss is aware of it or not. You do not set out to teach your child that temper tantrums will get them their own way. However, they learn that lesson if you buy them sweets when they start crying in the supermarket. Likewise, your boss will not deliberately teach you that putting forward new ideas will not pay. You will soon learn that lesson if every new idea you put forward is rejected because 'we've never done it before'. Your staff will learn to behave in a particular way because of the way you reward or punish types of behaviour. It is important for you to be aware of the things you are teaching them so that you can use this power to teach positive lessons and not negative ones.

Challenge. No development takes place until you are testing the upper level of performance. Give people a challenge and they will have to develop new skills and abilities to meet it.

How to be a Good Coach

1   *Look for learning opportunities.* The workplace is seething with learning opportunities for staff to develop their potential. Any business problem provides an opportunity for someone to solve it. You are unable to attend a meeting. Excellent, an opportunity to send a deputy who will benefit from the experience.

2   *Listen, don't lecture.* Resist the temptation to tell someone how to solve a problem that they have come up against. Listen to them explaining the problem and listen to how they intend to solve it. Do not take the problem back or explain to them how to solve it – they will not learn by following your solution, they will learn by working out their own.

3   *Ask questions, don't give answers.* If you must talk, then ask questions. Get your staff to think for themselves by using probing, open questions to examine motives, alternatives and the reasoning process which led to their conclusions. Questions like 'Why did you do it that way?', 'What alternatives did you discard?' and 'How will the customer react to that?' should guide the trainee into the questions he should be asking himself without giving him the answer. Too many managers fail to develop their staff because they see them as a tame audience for their pet theories on how to handle every problem. This is fine if you want a group of clones working for you but don't kid yourself that you are developing them.

4   *Set clear aims.* Tell people why they are doing things and what you expect from them. Explain where their task fits into the whole picture.

5 *Give clear feedback.* We have already explored the importance of recognizing and praising good work. One additional point is that in order to be most effective, feedback should be given immediately. Imagine a comedian waiting until the end of the act before getting applause or laughter. He would find it difficult to carry on. Give immediate feedback rather than save it up for the annual appraisal. Also, remember that no response is less helpful than a negative response, leaving the individual in limbo, unsure of whether they are a saint or a sinner.

Delegation

Delegation, and not love, makes the world go round. All organizations are based on delegation. Without it the chairman would be sweeping the warehouse while the warehouse assistant watches him (apparently this chairman came up the hard way and established an early reputation for being a terrific sweeper-up).

Delegation does two things:

- It improves a manager's own time planning by enabling him to hand over parts of his job.

- It develops the subordinate by enabling him to tackle more complex work.

Delegation is an important skill. Good delegators give themselves more time and their staff more challenge. Bad delegators create more problems for themselves and give their staff more headaches. The difference between being a good and a bad delegator is not too difficult to bridge. There are, however, several reasons why managers fail to delegate or delegate badly:

- They are afraid to give up control of part of their job whilst retaining responsibility if things go wrong.

- They like to hold on to the parts of the job that they enjoy, even though those bits could be done by a subordinate.

- They do not have the time to delegate.

- They have no one to delegate to.

- They delegate but either keep too tight a hold on the

work or abandon all responsibility for it.

- They forget to train the person to do the work that they want them to do.

- They delegate too much at once and swamp the person to whom they are delegating.

- They cannot tolerate someone doing a job in a different way from the way they would do it.

Managers who fail to delegate are often afraid to do so because of some problem in the past, caused by poor delegation. Delegation needs to be tackled systematically and gradually; it must be managed by you because whatever you delegate will remain your responsibility. It is part of your job that you are delegating and you will still be held responsible for it. That is not a reason for avoiding delegation, only for making sure that you delegate effectively. My Seven Point Plan for potential delegators should help you in this.

Step 1 — Examine your job
Look carefully at your job. Are you the most appropriate person to do every bit of it? Or are there parts of the job which someone else could do? Don't just pick out the dross, those things which you hate doing. Consider whole chunks of your job, include the things which you enjoy doing, and see if someone else can do them.

Step 2 — Consider your staff
Is there anyone who works for you who would benefit from taking on some of your work? Are they ready now or will they need some training? Do not delegate work to someone who could not do it – that would cause you more problems and, probably, damage their confidence and make them less likely to take on new work in future. If you have no one ready to delegate to, then consider how you can develop someone quickly. If all your staff are not ready to take on higher quality work, it points to an unimaginative manager. People often point to good managers and say 'He's OK, he's got good staff around him, the lucky b . . . .' My answer is that staff working for a good delegator look good themselves. They have been developed in the right way. Effective, well motivated staff reflect on their manager and so do lazy demotivated employees. The army used to say, 'There are no

bad soldiers, only bad officers.' How very true!

Step 3 — Consult

If you can match the work with the person, discuss your proposals with them. The 'I have decided to give you X' approach is nowhere near as effective as the 'I've been thinking. Do you feel that you can tackle X?' approach. If they agree, explain the work thoroughly and tell them what standards you expect from them. Remember that you delegate authority and not responsibility and explain that to them.

Step 4 — Agree a handover

Agree a sensible timetable for handing work over. Avoid dumping it at one fell swoop. Feed it to them slowly but not so slowly that they find it boring but, conversely, not so quickly that they find it overwhelming. Keep the timetable flexible so that if they pick things up quicker or slower than you expect you can adjust their programme.

Step 5 — Inform

Ensure that the people who need to know are fully informed and that they know that they should direct problems at the person with the authority. This will boost the confidence of the delegate and direct time-consuming problems away from you. If they try to delegate problems back up to you, do not accept them. Ask them what they propose to do with the problem and guide them by asking probing questions about the solutions they describe.

Step 6 — Train

Make sure that you train staff in any part of the job which is not clear to them. Firstly, it is essential that they understand what they are doing. Secondly, lack of training is often used as an excuse by an under-confident member of staff to hand back a chunk of delegated work. Train them in fairness to both themselves and you.

Step 7 — Monitor

There are two possible sins at this stage. The Hovering Boss syndrome and the Spartan Baby syndrome.

The Hovering Boss delegates a piece of work and then spends the next few hours asking how it is coming along and giving unasked for advice. Give people a chance to get on with the job in their own way and accept that their way may not necessarily be an exact replica of yours.

The Spartan Baby syndrome gets its name from the custom of the Spartans which involved leaving babies out in the cold for a period to ensure that only the strong survived. Macho managers believe that you should give people a job to do, let them get on with it (without training) and let them sink or swim. This gets rid of the wimps and ensures that only the strong managers survive. The 'sink or swim' theory has a few weak points:

- Even the strongest swimmer can drown in heavy seas.

- Swimmers about to enter the sea lose their confidence at the sight of other swimmers drowning.

- Managers who believe in the 'sink or swim' ethic spend more time saving drowning men or burying corpses than they would in teaching people to swim.

Monitor carefully but don't over-monitor. Give clear feedback, help them deal with problems but avoid taking the problems back. Then you can concentrate on what to do with the time you save by delegating.

Some Specific Ideas for Coaches

Some of these are things which can come under the heading of delegation, some are more specific ideas for the coach. Coaching is cost-effective – all you need is a trainee and the workplace. Not only do you develop new skills and abilities, you can provide the managers of the future whilst solving some of today's business problems and exploiting some real live business opportunities.

Projects: Every area of every business has those jobs which everyone intends to get round to 'sometime'. They must be a challenging learning opportunity for if they were easy to solve, someone would have done it. They are a job for someone (normally we hear *'someone* should improve the layout of this warehouse' or *'someone* should look into improving our grocery range') and an ideal opportunity for development and improvement of the way things are done.

Accompanying the boss: Part of developing people is broadening their perspective, allowing them to look at the way things are done at a higher level. This can be done by inviting them to accompany you to meetings and visits. They have the opportunity to observe and you have the opportunity to give a 'pre-match briefing' or a debriefing after the event. What they observe coupled with your commentary on the events will probably prove to be a useful learning experience. They, however, need to be trained in the skills of observation so that they know what to look for.

Deputizing: Even more active learning is gained from deputizing for the boss. If you are unable to attend a meeting, instead of sending apologies, send a deputy – one who will benefit from the experience. If there are some matters that you wish to raise, let him raise them instead of leaving them until the next meeting. Brief the chairman of the meeting that you will be sending a deputy, so that your deputy is correctly introduced and encouraged to speak. Again, make sure that they are well briefed and that the experience is fully reviewed.

Secondments: Planning experience is an important factor in development rather than leaving an individual's career to the vagaries of the internal vacancy system. An engineer may need some feel for marketing if he is in the product development area; then he should be seconded to a marketing department with a specific project to do. If a grocery manager is barred from developing because he has no experience in working with fresh foods, then his boss should arrange a secondment so that he can run a fresh food department.

Managing in microcosm: In order to allow an individual to see a microcosm of a larger job, it is often possible to give them a particular section of your own work where they are totally responsible and where they carry out all the parts of your job but on a smaller scale. A grocery buyer can develop a junior by giving them a small section, such as breakfast cereals, where they carry out all the negotiating, product development and so on. Of course the area needs to be selected with care.

Planned reading: Many books on management or specialized topics give guidance and information to young managers. Any books which you find useful, you should note down and pass the information on. If you know that your staff are reading a book ask them about it, discuss it and get them to think about its implications for what they are doing.

Self Development Activities

1   Think back over your own career. Which managers helped

138 BE THE MOST EFFECTIVE MANAGER IN YOUR BUSINESS

you the most? How did they do it?

2   Make a list of problems and opportunities in your area that you have not been able to focus your attention on. Can you ask a member of your staff to handle them or can you delegate some work so that you can handle them? Draw up an action plan to put this into effect.

23
Dealing with the Poor Performer

Dealing with performers who are below standard is an important part of any manager's job. Doing the terribly nice things like coaching and delegation are relatively painless but dealing with the problem children can be a difficult and stressful process for both parties. There are two types of manager whose approach to discipline is unproductive:

- *The ostrich.* The manager who refuses to face up to a performance problem and who, when he finally admits its existence, cannot bear to confront the person concerned.

- *The hatchet man.* Some managers delight in dealing with performance problems. They consider that anyone who is not doing the job to the required standard is automatically at fault and thus should be dismissed.

Obviously both of these approaches are extremes. The ostrich's problem will not go away. It will only increase as his good workers see that problems are not dealt with and thus lose the incentive to produce high quality work themselves. The hatchet man will sack many good workers who just happen to be going through a difficult phase or who are in the wrong job.

There are several principles which need to be kept in mind when dealing with a case of poor performance.

- Procrastination does not help a problem, it only makes it worse.

- Poor performance left untreated is contagious, it can go through a whole department.

- Poor performers are often good performers in the wrong environment.

- Every problem has a cause. Discover the cause and you will be closer to finding a solution.

- Competent people do not become incompetent overnight.

The manager is responsible for maintaining standards of performance in his own area. It is not a matter for personnel or any other advisor, although they may make helpful suggestions about the setting and enforcing of these standards. The manager's responsibilities can be summarized as follows:

- *Setting the standard.* The first responsibility of the manager is to determine what is acceptable performance. What standards of cleanliness are needed in the factory? What level of sales is required from each salesman? This is an integral part of the manager's job, deciding what level of performance he will accept from his staff. That standard must be:
  Achievable – not unrealistically high.
  Challenging – not pathetically low.
  Consistent – applicable at any time and not related to the manager's current mood.
  Universal – applying to all staff not just those with blue eyes.

- *Communicating the standard.* Now that you have clarified the standard you require, inform your staff. Spell out what you expect from them and ensure that they understand it. If you do this and give them clear feedback on their performance in relation to that standard, then much of the performance problem will become self-regulating and staff will be able to measure their own performance. Your involvement will then focus on solving the problem, not on whether the problem actually exists. Disciplinary interviews which start with an argument about which standards exist and a debate about whether they have been breached or not are missing the point. These facts should be incontrovertible.

- *Enforcing the standard.* Do not duck the problems. If

performance drops below the standard then do not allow it to continue without discussing it with the individual concerned. It is fair to both sides – yourself because you are judged by the performance of your staff; the performer because they will know that their performance is slipping and will be waiting in anguish for you to call them in.

The Disciplinary Interview

How do people describe the disciplinary interview that they are about to go into?

'I'm going to have it out with him.'

'There are going to be a few straight words this afternoon.'

'I shall sort him out once and for all.'

'I'm going to have a little talk with her.' (This last phrase is usually said in a tone thick with menace.)

The scene is set for 'Showdown at the OK Corral'. Everything is quiet, too quiet. The parties are armed, either with damning facts or undeniable alibis. The word has gone round that there is a showdown coming and expectations are high, the air dripping with tension. There is pressure on the manager to do something decisive, an equally firm pressure on the victim to tell that so-and-so a thing or two. I defy anyone to come up with a constructive solution to a performance problem under these circumstances.

It need not be like this. It is this atmosphere of confrontation which pushes managers into the role of either sheriff (shooting first, asking questions later) or the town coward ('OK boys, I want you to go on home and cause no trouble here'). There are several things to bear in mind about disciplinary interviews which reduce tension and produce sensible results.

- It is a meeting to resolve a problem not a courtroom. You want better performance; in most cases, so do they. Listen carefully to their problems, probe them gently. They may be telling you the cause and solution of the problem.

- Don't make the meeting public or even public knowledge. Try to make sure that you are not the one to publicize it and encourage the interviewee not to do so. At least initially, make it a discussion, not a formal interview, unless you are dealing with a serious breach of discipline which is being processed through a formal procedure.

- Ensure that both parties leave the interview committed to a positive action plan. Also agree when this will be reviewed and make sure that you keep to your part of the commitment.

- End the interview on a positive note and when it is over do not bear a grudge. Many managers get so uptight about discipline interviews that they behave like John McEnroe for the rest of the day.

Thinking about the Unthinkable

Do not keep someone in a job who cannot perform in it. Consider creative alternatives with your personnel department – transfer, re-training, demotion and so on – but if they cannot do the job and dismissal is the only option, don't let your finer feelings stop you. But, avoid cruelty or vindictiveness. Do it in a humane way. Remember that your poor performer may be someone else's dream performer.

Self Development Activities

1   Write down your understanding of the standards of performance expected of you by your boss. Then go on to clarify what you are expecting of your staff.

24
What Makes a Successful Team?

Is it possible for a man to be a great strategic thinker and yet be able to consider minute detail? Or be an ideas man and yet a cold, clinical evaluator? Or to be an expert on production, personnel and finance? It is possible but it is also highly unlikely. One person cannot do and be everything but a team can or, at least, it can combine all the main areas of skill and knowledge that are needed for a particular job. That is why so many of our working lives are spent in teams of one type or another – working parties, task forces, project teams, committees and so on.

This chapter is devoted to the team, bringing it together, getting the right number and the right mix. A group of people can become an effective team, sharing common aims and having a strong bond or it can remain a group which meets, talks and disagrees. A manager needs to know the difference between a group and a team and how to make a group into a team. There is no doubt that a team of less gifted individuals will always defeat a group made up of all the talents who are unable to come together effectively.

What is a Team?

A team quite simply is 'a number of individuals working together to achieve a common task'. This definition brings out some important factors:

- *A number of individuals* – Teamwork should bring individuals together in such a way that they increase their effectiveness without losing their individuality. For example, an orchestra is a team made up of brilliant individualists. They are not expected to perform beneath their standard but the conductor attempts to blend each individual's performance together in order to make a superlative team performance.

their standard but the conductor attempts to blend each individual's performance together in order to make a superlative team performance.

The secret of effective teamwork is to find the role for each instrument for which it is suited. If the instrument is playing a role which fits in with its range and tone, this is ideal. To ask an instrument to play beyond its range is foolish and to ask an instrument to play too far within its range is not making full use of available resources.

In the same way the members of a business team should consist of individuals who together can be more effective than they are working alone. They should also be asked to take on a role which fits their particular skills and abilities, thereby enhancing their individuality rather than suppressing it.

- *Working together* – A team must work together or else it remains a group. If the individuals are not brought together by a leader or a manager they remain individuals. The orchestra needs a conductor, or at least some way of making sure that they are all playing the same piece at the same tempo.

- *To achieve a common task* – The task and its objectives must be commonly agreed and understood. The task may be active or passive, offensive or defensive, important or trivial but it *must* be common to the team and clearly communicated and understood by the team.

  In the field of politics, it is fascinating how individuals from different parties can form an effective team if they are working together to achieve a common task. Churchill's war cabinet was an effective team even though it was made up of politicians from all three parties because it was working hard in the same task. However, after the General Election of 1945, the members of the war cabinet rejoined their old party organization and fell back into the 'old ways' of government and opposition because they ceased to share the same objectives.

  A business team needs to be brought together to share a common task and this is one of the important skills of leadership. Project teams consisting of marketing, production, accountancy and personnel have to be convinced that the task that they are sharing transcends their departmental loyalties. Many interdisciplinary project groups have foundered on the rock of departmental jealousy because the aims of their new team have remained subordinate to those of their functional departments.

Synergy

I have tried to avoid using jargon in this book. However, there is one important piece of jargon which aptly describes the power of teams. It is a word borrowed from the biological sciences – 'synergy'. It describes the phenomenon in which the combined activity of separate entities has a greater effect than the sum of the activities of each entity working alone.

OK, simple English. If one man takes one hour to build a brick wall, how long will it take two men? The mathematical answer is half an hour but the bricklayer's answer would be twenty minutes. Why? The reason is synergy. Synergy operates not just by reducing the time to carry out the task in proportion to the number of people working on it; it also has the effect of improving the quality of work of the participants by better organization and a more fertile flow of ideas.

Synergy depends, however, on a common purpose. If this agreement is not present then the two men may take two hours to build a brick wall or, indeed, may never finish it at all.

How Many?

Sporting teams provide us with a clear guide to the right number for a team. Most major sports regulate teams to between six and fifteen. A tennis doubles partnership is not a team nor were the two tribes who played in the football match in *Tom Brown's Schooldays*. A team needs to be small enough to enable the leader to keep in touch with the whole team but large enough to enable each individual to play an effective role without being swamped by the boss.

In the fields of sport and politics, two areas where competitiveness has honed teamwork to a sharp cutting edge, we can see excellent examples of team numbers finding their own level. Sports which allow for teams of more than eleven tend to break down into more manageable chunks. For example, Rugby Union teams have a captain for the full quota of fifteen players but because the squad is likely to be spread all over the pitch in two separate formations, a leader is usually appointed to lead the scrum, which is a team within a team. The pack leader has, in effect, powers delegated to him by the team captain because he is always with the pack of forwards and if the captain is a member of the back line, there are places where he would be unable to go.

Political groupings are another example of groups reducing to teams of an appropriate size for the task in hand. The constitutional researcher would stress that most cabinets have twenty or thirty members, some contain up to fifty members. Cabinets are large because they need to accommodate the leaders of a wide range of ministerial teams and also because they need to accommodate all the factions of a political party. This unwieldiness has caused many problems for prime ministers, presidents and commissars. The formal cabinet group is thus usually far from being a cohesive team, including, as it often does, all the prime minister's political rivals, and so when a team is needed – in particular to meet a crisis – the cabinet usually develops a small 'inner cabinet' of six or seven members. In most moments of crisis, prime ministers usually put their faith in teamwork and even under normal circumstances, major decisions are usually made by a small team of like-minded advisors.

During the Falklands crisis, the Prime Minister's team included regularly no more than seven or eight members, all of whom had specific expertise.

In business organizations, large unwieldy committees are often effectively replaced by small cohesive teams. Michael Edwardes cut back the British Leyland board to six, of whom only three were executive members.

Military organizations, such as the Roman army, worked in groups of ten, preferring to keep the teams cohesive even though this may increase the number of levels in the hierarchy.

The question has to be asked, 'Is there an optimum size for a team?' The answer depends on the situation in which the team is expected to perform. There are a number of factors which need to be taken into account.

- *The appropriate level of conflict within the group.* Mathematically, the odds of conflict arising between two members of a group must increase with the number in the group.

    However, a small group is more likely to be dominated by the views of one strong member, especially the type of leader who recruits in his or her own image. This means that the group may not be giving consideration to the alternative methods of achieving their objectives.

    A job which needs to be done quickly and effectively needs the minimum of conflict. However, a long-term project with far-reaching consequences may need the variety of opinions and ideas which a large group would generate.

- *The variety of expertise required.* A major technological project may require a large number of experts. A simple project may need a small team to oversee it. If a large body of knowledge is required and a large team brought together the team leader needs to be aware of the problems that a large caucus can cause and try to break the team into cohesive subgroups as quickly as possible. It is more effective to create a small hierarchy than to run a large unwieldy committee.

- *The level of expertise of the leader.* In a small working group of three or four, the leader can become so expert in the work of all the group that his supervision becomes suffocating, overwhelming the individuality of group members. At the other end of the scale, a group can be so large that the leader can't take even a passing interest in the work of his team. Without the motivation of the leader's apparent interest and enthusiasm for their part of the job, individuals can become disillusioned and apathetic.

- *The physical proximity of the team.* All other things being equal, the further apart the members of a team are located, the smaller the team should be. Communication problems grow with distance and can only be more complicated with more people in the network.

Although it is difficult to be specific about the ideal number for an effective team, nevertheless certain numbers recur when successful teams are analysed. Teams with more than ten or eleven members often need to be broken down into sub-groups.

Teams with fewer than three or four members tend to become dominated by one man and often cannot provide the variety of technical or managerial experience required to do the job.

At the other extreme, many companies in line production industries have had great success in experiments which reduce the number of employees reporting to one man. One company found that a foreman was supervising fifty staff; little wonder that he felt harrassed and they felt unnoticed. They solved the problem by introducing five chargehands who each had nine staff working for them. This reform meant that no team had more than ten members. Even with the introduction of an additional level in the hierarchy, communication increased and output rose. From a wandering herd the fifty men had become a sharper, well-motivated group of teams.

Getting the Right Mix

If a team is to be successful it has to be carefully selected to ensure that the right skills, both technical and process, are available.

Unfortunately, many managers recruit in their own image. 'Send in the clones' a colleague of mine used to call it. The principle which underpins this phenomenon is 'What this Company/Department/Section needs is more people like me.' Managers select similarly minded team members or people with similar personal qualities, often in order to reduce the potential for conflict within the team. In fact, by recruiting people whose roles are likely to overlap because of their similar personalities, they are increasing the likelihood of conflict.

A team needs the right blend if it is to be more effective than a group of individuals. It needs to be composed of people with a wide range of strengths – both technical and managerial. By selecting a team carefully a manager can have access to a wide range of technical and personal skills which give an all round perspective to the work he is doing.

A well selected team can also ensure that there is little or no overlap of roles, with all members of the team making an effective contribution in an area where they are strong and feeling confident that their areas of weakness are covered by the strengths of their colleagues. In a well rounded team, people use their strengths to best effect, this adds to their confidence and adds to the feeling of team spirit which is an important factor in a team's success. It is important to achieve a blend of abilities in two main areas – technical abilities and team roles.

In major projects the team carrying out the work must make sure it possesses as much technical information from as many sources as necessary. Management teams which are dominated by a particular function tend to produce results which reflect that domination. So, decisions made by a production dominated group tend to reflect the interests of the production department, possibly leading to a beautifully crafted product that nobody wants to buy.

The second area, that of team roles, is not always given sufficient weight. Usually, the people with the technical expertise are available but little thought is given to bringing a team together which will have the correct blend of personal qualities and managerial behaviour.

Successful teams need people to play specific roles if they are to have a well balanced approach to their tasks. These roles cover the qualities of a 'supermanager', the person who can display incompatible characteristics at the same time; but instead of being an individual performing psychological contortions and trying to generate new ideas and evaluate them at the same time, the team has different members playing different roles – roles with which they are comfortable.

In selecting potentially successful teams, the effective manager doesn't just pick the cleverest people available; that sort of behaviour belongs in the school gym when picking teams for five-a-side football. The effective manager picks people who will work together, not in a cosy way but as a team, with personal qualities which provide a wide range of strengths which can be brought into play at particular stages. Research work has determined eight major roles in teams:

Chairman – provides the leadership function of keeping the team focused on the task objectives. He or she tries to bring out the team's combined resources as effectively as possible.

Driver – usually an aggressive extrovert, drives the team

towards the objectives. Highly competitive, he or she provides the impetus towards action but in doing so can walk over his/her colleagues.

Spark – provides the creative spark in the team; generates ideas at a fast pace and can often bring fresh insights into the team's work. Usually very intelligent.

Critic – provides the analysis of ideas and suggestions. Objective and rational, he or she prevents the team from getting carried away with impractical ideas.

Implementer – gets things from ideas to action methodically. He or she takes decisions and strategies and turns them into manageable tasks.

'Mr Fix It' – the person who knows everyone and where to get hold of everything. He or she has many contacts outside the team and is skilled at adapting other people's ideas.

Team builder – sensitive to the needs of the team and the maintainer of harmony.

Finisher – when other members of the team may be concerned with strategy, the finisher will be concerned to make sure that the details have been attended to.

The description of eight roles does not mean that a team cannot be effective with fewer than eight members. Members can adopt two or more roles if necessary. The research by Dr Belbin has shown that team members have roles in which they are most comfortable and roles which they can fulfil if necessary.

Looking at the roles, the consequences of the absence of one of these functions can have a great effect on the effectiveness of the team. With no spark, the team can get bogged down; with no finisher, important details can be missed; with no critic, the team can be swayed by the very bright, articulate and possibly impractical spark and so on.

Dr Belbin, who carried out the research on team roles, has developed tests for team members to help them review their roles. It is an important element in building a successful team, that the members of that team can identify themselves with a role and thus concentrate on the contribution they make to the team's performance.

Getting the mix right is vital, if the team is to be effective. The business world is full of unsuccessful teams made up of gifted individuals who are unable to work together.

Self Development Activities

1 Examine any team of which you are a member. Are there any weaknesses caused by not having someone in the team with the right technical or managerial perspective?

2 Examine your own team. Can you see a team role for each member?

3 Analyse the membership of successful teams in politics, exploration and sport. These activities are highly competitive and the membership of teams is of particular importance.

25
Leadership

We have already seen how an effective team needs to be made up of the right blend of abilities and personalities. We have also looked at some of the principles involved in managing individuals correctly. In addition to these, we have looked at techniques for carrying out particular tasks such as decision making, problem solving and handling negotiations. In this chapter, I am going to draw these three areas together and examine the manager's responsibility for the leadership of a team of individuals in carrying out their work.

One misconception that it is important to deal with at the start is the view that good leaders are born and not made. Whilst there are some personal qualities which predispose people to become leaders 'naturally'; leadership qualities can be learned and developed by anyone. Leaders with charisma are often less successful in the leadership role because they try less hard, feeling that their charisma will be enough to carry them through.

Management involves using resources to carry out a particular task. Those resources include people and the manager must learn to get the best out of those individuals. Leadership takes the management of people a stage further and is to do with the use and development of working teams. Leadership is the part of management which inspires people to work together to achieve tasks by releasing their potential and directing their energy.

Leadership brings together the areas that we have already discussed – the individual, the team and the job. A leader who is too concerned with developing individuals to the detriment of the team as a whole will not be effective. Likewise, a leader who submerges the rights of the individual under the flood of team spirit will lose the respect and mar the effectiveness of that individual. Of course, any leader who respects both the team and the individuals within it but who fails to achieve the task will also be seen as an ineffective manager. The individuals, the team and the task must all be taken into equal account if the leader is to be effective.

Leadership is a skill which can be developed by reflecting on your own experience and by considering the effective managers and leaders for whom you have worked. My own job involves running assessment centres for senior managers and one of the most difficult areas for observers to agree a common set of criteria is that of leadership. It is often easier to say what it isn't:

- Leadership is not autocracy although autocrats can also be good leaders. The skills of leadership are not those of dominating people but of enabling them to bring out their best performance. Of course, leadership must involve high standards and discipline; but the great leaders have the ability to raise morale and to generate commitment. It is easy for managers with strong personalities to dominate their staff; it is a great skill to get a group of people to produce high quality work.

- Leadership is not automatically guaranteed by holding a particular position. Authority can be conferred by your role in a company or by acquiring specialized skills. Neither of these are effective in a leadership role without the personal authority to use them. In an organizational context, a leader can always manage; a manager may not always be able to lead.

Leadership Style

Genghis Khan, Mahatma Gandhi, Stalin, Jesus Christ, Napoleon, Moses, John Kennedy – all were leaders who made their mark on the world. That is the only thing that they had in common. Their various approaches to leadership cover the whole spectrum – from cruelty to gentleness; from autocracy to participation.

There is no one route to leadership, although effective leaders do share some qualities and do carry out similar functions. The same job can be carried out equally effectively by different people with contrasting styles.

There are a number of factors which influence a manager's style of leadership. Some elements of style are specific to the person; some to the situation. A leader must learn to be flexible without being inconsistent and firm without being autocratic.

Natural style: There are certain personal qualities which can predetermine a manager's style of leadership. Contrast the prime ministerial styles of Attlee and Macmillan; the former a quiet introvert, the latter an articulate and flamboyant showman, and yet both strong and effective leaders. Effective leaders remain true to their own natural style. The most important analysis that a leader can make is a self-analysis of strengths and weaknesses and the likely impact of this on their team.

Situation: Certain situations require different leadership from others. These can be measured on a scale ranging from highly directive to highly participative. Factors which can affect the position on the scale can include time constraint, complexity and the amount of risk involved. In warfare, the planning of a battle may be carried out by a general by consulting with his subordinates, but in the middle of a battle, the leadership style must be highly directive.

Organizational culture: Organizations vary in the amount of authority they allow managers and the style of leadership which is acceptable. Highly unionized organizations tend to be participative in an increasing number of business areas. Other companies tend to be directive and highly centralized. A directive manager in a participative company will find life particularly difficult, because his style will be seen as particularly aggressive in comparison with his more easygoing colleagues.

'Age' of the team: An experienced team will need less direct leadership than a newly formed team. A leader will need to guide a new team more consciously than a more experienced team, like individual delegation a team needs to be eased into a task rather than thrown into it. If a leader sets a high standard and then leaves a team to work on it, they may get confused and a new leader will fill what is seen as a vacuum. Participative leadership should not be an abdication of leadership.

What Does a Leader Do?

What does a leader do? Many managers who should be playing a leadership role find it difficult because they are not sure what it is. We understand what work is; we see people do it and what they produce. We find it more difficult to understand what management and leadership is, because the output which is produced is intangible. A car mechanic fixes a damaged gear box, we see clearly what he is doing; his foreman is walking around the garage giving work to other people, we know what he is doing although it doesn't look much like work to us; the garage manager is sitting in his office thinking, we don't know what he is doing or thinking and, what is more, we find it hard to measure his effectiveness.

The leader should not take on a leadership role for the kudos, it is rare that any credit comes that way. If the leader has done an effective job, it will be the team members who gain the credit because their performance, which is more easily measured, will rise perceptibly. If the team fails, then the leader will be blamed. A good example of this is the performance of the England cricket team. A victory and the headline refers to the successful batsmen or bowlers; a defeat and the captain is blamed.

The sports analogy leads to the question, 'Should the captain always be the best player?' All management thinkers would reply with a resounding 'No!' In fact the best player is often the person who should not be captain. It is a rare gift for the most talented sportman to be also the most inspiring leader. In fact the team often suffers when the star is the captain, someone whose performance is so crucial to the team's success cannot also be thinking about the performance of the rest of the team. Leadership, like captaincy, is a skill and should be regarded as such. The skill is that of enabling others to perform to their best ability. If the leader is successful in this, the credit will go to the team member whose performance has been enhanced.

The leader therefore is usually not the person with the greatest job knowledge. It is, however, hard to be a leader without understanding the job, especially for the supervisor or first line manager. It is important to understand the team's task in order to set sensible objectives but not necessarily to know everybody else's job in the company. The chairman of

ICI doesn't need to be a chemist (the current chairman isn't) but he has to understand the business of manufacturing chemicals.

The leader has to know enough of the job to set standards. 'Walking the job' is important to maintaining those standards and an effective leader has to be seen regularly at the workplace in order to spot problems and sense atmospheres. We shall see later that effective leaders are in high profile and keeping an eye on things fulfils that objective too.

The area in which the leader makes a major contribution to both the task and the team is in directing and communicating the aims of the group. This is why it is important for the leader to understand the team's task expertise but not be so immersed in the detail of the task that the overall objectives and their place within the organization are forgotten.

The functions of a leader therefore can be summarized as follows:

1   The leader is often responsible for either setting the aims for the team or clarifying those aims. Leadership in a large organization is carried out at a number of levels; some of those levels are responsible for setting aims for the team and at some levels aims are passed down and clarified for their team. This is providing the common task which we said in the previous chapter helped to define a team.

Even if the aims which are passed down are vague and poorly articulated, the team leader is responsible for making them clear and achievable. A team without clearly measurable aims cannot be expected to function as a team.

2   The leader leads a team and also in large organizations acts as the representative of senior management, providing the route of communication from other levels in the organization to the team. This can be an onerous role. The leader of one team is usually a member of a team of team leaders and so on. Much of the communication from above will come through their leader and they may not always agree with it. However, each member of that team will have to pass on company policy as if they fully agreed with it. A leader not only has to communicate information and decisions but has to generate the commitment of the team to those decisions. This commitment cannot be generated by introducing company policy with statements like, 'You won't believe the latest nonsense that Head Office have come up with.'

The leader's task is not only to keep the team together but to keep the team cemented to the whole organization. The aims that the team are set need to be put into the context of the organization's activities by the leader, who is responsible for explaining clearly the corporate objectives.

3   If there are any faults in comunication in a group then the leader is to blame. Clarifying the aims and putting them in a wider context can only be done by organizing clear and regular communication sessions. Regular information sessions on both the team's tasks and the progress of the business as a whole must be communicated in order that the team is fully aware and is unable to blame the leader for keeping them in the dark. There is a great thirst for communication in any organization; if it is not provided by the leadership, then it will be provided by the informal grapevine of rumour and half-truths.

Communication must be planned regularly and should be done on a team basis, not by mentioning things to individuals and hoping that the message will get around. Playing 'Chinese whispers' is no substitute for well organized team meetings where information and opinion flows two ways. Managers who are concerned at the prospect of calling and chairing meetings should read chapter 17.

4   Communication is not just the process of transmitting information as quickly as possible. It is partly a process of gaining the commitment of the team to the task. Commitment needs to be generated in order to ensure that the team not only carry out the task but that they carry out the task with enthusiasm. There is a visible difference between a team doing the bare minimum and one working hard to achieve stretching objectives. The difference is not usually in the team but in the leader. Workgroups previously regarded as problem children suddenly become a well-motivated team with a new leader. They have not changed, the leadership is the key. History is full of armies which are transformed from a dispirited mob to an elite corps by a new general. The ability to raise a team's performance is a necessary condition of effective leadership.

5   Once the aims of the task have been clarified and communicated, the leader cannot sit back and await the laurel crown. The team needs continuing direction to ensure that it stays on track. The leader guides the team through the planning and activity of the task, not by telling individuals

exactly how to play their role but by continuing to emphasize the purpose and to ensure that progress is made towards meeting the success criteria which had been set at the beginning.

6   In order to ensure that the team remains united behind the aims, the leader has to pay attention to the team's shared needs. If a team can work better than a group of purposeless individuals, then it is the leader who must pay attention to keeping that team together. In the previous chapter, we saw' some of the factors which make an effective team – size and diversity. The leader may be able to structure the team to fit the task but more often may have to carry out the task with a team that was established for some other purpose. Whatever the situation, the leader has to take the raw materials and build them into an effective team.

7   We said in the previous chapter that a team is a group of individuals. Team spirit is an important factor in achieving success but it is important that the needs of the individual are always recognized. No individual is greater than the team but each individual has a right to be respected and recognized for the part that they play. The team will only function well when all the members are playing their role effectively; those members will only perform effectively when they are clear about the role that they are expected to play and how that role fits into the team objectives. The leader needs to get to know each team member well, especially their strengths and weaknesses, so that each individual is able to use their strengths and minimize their weaknesses. This will create a strong team of individuals who are confident of their ability in the role they are expected to play. An unfulfilled individual will always detract from the effectiveness of the team.

8   One particularly important role is the selection and induction of new members in the team. It is unlikely that teams are selected and then remain unchanged throughout. Teams grow and reduce with members joining and leaving all the time. Selection of a new member is a difficult task. The effective leader will look for someone whose strengths complement the portfolio of abilities currently available to the team. The wrong decision at this stage would be to recruit a 'clone' of another effective team member – two people with the same abilities are very likely to produce unproductive conflict. The new member must fit into the existing team and be

prepared to act as a member of that team.

The leader must ensure that the new member develops an understanding of the team aims and their role within the team as quickly as possible. The other team members must not be neglected during this phase. If the new member is a high-flier, then be very careful how they are inducted into the team. They must not be seen as having been brought in to remedy some problem in the team, otherwise the existing members will not co-operate with them and harmony will be destroyed.

9 Teams consist of individuals with personalities, emotions and a variety of interests; it is not inconceivable that there will be times when these individuals disagree. Disagreement is not at all disturbing, in fact a team that did not disagree would not be an effective one. Disagreements resulting from new ideas and team members suggesting alternative methods of working are positive signs of an effect- ive team. They should be welcomed and even encouraged.

However, when these disagreements arise from more funda- mental issues they begin to fall in the category of conflict. Conflict is negative and is a regressive force which dilutes effective teamwork and prevents achievement of aims. Conflict arises when people feel that they are being threatened and are about to lose something which they value – status, beliefs and ideals, resources and the priority of their work.

The effects of conflict are either overt or covert. Aggression is the most easily observed, where team members argue a point and follow the traditional pattern in which either a winner or loser emerges or a compromise is finally reached. Other effects can be hidden aggression, which is basically lack of co-operation or absenteeism, and broadening the fight into other team members' areas. The leader has a responsibility for preventing or handling conflict in a team. This can be a very stressful role as it may involve the leader in a great deal of emotion. In fact, the leader may find himself the target for aggression.

Conflict can be hidden or immediately apparent. Many leaders who would regard themselves as peacemakers take the view that conflict is better left hidden. Provided that things are calm on the surface, all is well. This is, of course, untrue. Doctors will confirm that unrelieved tension can be a cause of almost every major disease. Disagreements should be aired openly before they are allowed to degenerate into conflict.

In order to do this, the leader has to create an open atmosphere in which team members are encouraged to express ideas and emotions openly. This free expression is a positive force for high quality work. The leader has to be assertive and to encourage the team to express themselves in the same way. Assertiveness is an adult way of forceful self-expression without aggression. It assumes mutual respect and removes the need to indulge in either 'fight' or 'flight' behaviour which the aggression/submission cycle enforces.

10   A leader will be forgiven almost any error when leading a successful team. Organizations allow successful teams to run themselves, preferring to concentrate on those which are performing badly. Success feeds on success. When a team is successful the leader must feed that success back to the team: all other things being equal, this will create more success. Successful teams can become more successful until they become complacent.

The Characteristics of a Leader

We started this chapter by saying that there were an infinite range of personality types which were appropriate for leadership but that effective leaders carried out certain functions. It is also true to say that all effective leaders possess certain characteristics whatever other traits they might also possess. The list below is not exhaustive!

1   Integrity and loyalty to the team. If a team is to be united in a task behind a leader, it is essential that they have faith in that leader. For them to have faith, the leader must treat them honestly and fairly. If the leader is to set, clarify and communicate the team's aims, they must believe in the veracity of that communication. The leader must also represent the team when dealing with senior managers and directors and defend the team loyally if the need arises. Nothing gives a team more determination than knowing that their leader is fighting for them in the boardroom.

2   Allied to loyalty and integrity are openness and firmness. The leaders should strive to create an atmosphere where the whole team works frankly and openly with each other. Secret cabals and sub-groups are counter-productive to the working of an effective team. The leader must also have a reputation for demanding high standards of the team – 'firm

but fair' has become a cliché but many people use it to describe their most effective boss.

3   John Adair in his book *Effective Leadership* quotes Lord Slim, commander of the 14th Army in Burma, who when asked how a leader taught integrity to his team answered, 'By example.' If the manager is seen to be a 'wide boy' (or wide girl, of course), fiddling expenses, skating on thin ice with the company's policy book and generally acting in a devious way, this will not encourage the team to be honest.

4   The effective leader possesses helicopter ability, the skill of hovering above the task to ensure that the task is being achieved and to review the team's effectiveness. The engineer who loves to get stuck into a technical problem may often miss other things which are happening in the plant. A leader needs antennae for problems, especially people problems, and needs to keep above the day-to-day work wherever possible. The captain of an ocean liner who kept rushing off to check the temperature of the soup in the mess when the ship was in heavy seas would almost certainly be relieved of his command. His job would be at the bridge, not necessarily steering, just watching.

5   The effective leader keeps it simple. All the great leaders communicate their message to their followers in a simple way. Jesus Christ consolidated the complex Mosaic law into two simple mission statements 'Love God' and 'Love thy neighbour as thyself'. Many managers fear simplicity, they like to over-complicate. They fear that people may say that if things are too simple then who needs a manager to explain them? Simplicity is a virtue and if a concept is explained simply, then human communication is at its most effective.

6   Enthusiasm. The effective manager seeks not only compliance but commitment. It is easy to bully people into carrying out a task somehow; it is a leadership skill to persuade people to carry out a task with commitment. It is hard to expect a team to be committed if the leader is unenthusiastic. The leader has to show enthusiasm and to transfer this commitment to the team. Enthusiasm is contagious; it affects the people that it touches.

Self Development Activities

1   Read about, observe and analyse effective leaders in

action. What makes them effective? How does their style match the task that they have to do?

2   Observe your own team. Stand back and watch them in action. Instead of chairing one of your own meetings, ask someone else to do it and watch your team objectively.

26
Managing Change

One of my first assignments on joining a retail company was to draw up a short training programme on 'Handling Change'. I researched the topic thoroughly and made my recommendations. The manager who had asked me to carry out the assignment looked blank as I presented them. He finally said, 'When do you get to the introduction of the pound coin?.' I looked blankly at him and the penny dropped. I had worked long and hard on the process of change, the manager wanted to train check-out operators in the gentle art of handing back money to customers.

Managers still do not think of managing change as a major issue in their job. In today's world, though, it has become a subject which every manager should think carefully about because the working environment and the social environment are changing much more than ever. The manager must not only be able to adapt to change himself but must also be able to explain change to his staff and to motivate them to adapt to change.

The books of Alvin Toffler describe the massive changes which are taking place in our society now. Every manager should read the books because they are stimulating and readable. Changes which take place in technology lead to changes in environment, lifestyle, the community and the family. The effective manager is aware of these changes and adapts to them rather than fights against them. There are three perspectives on change which I want to deal with here:

- Living with change.

- Preparing staff for change.

- Handling changes in your own career.

Living with Change

Life is becoming more volatile. The pace of change is accelerating and many of our social and medical problems are related to inability to adapt to this pace. Alvin Toffler clearly explains this acceleration by his explanation of the 800th lifetime; if we divide man's existence on the planet into lifetimes, we are now on the 800th and during this lifetime more has changed than in the whole of the previous 799. Look around you: how many of the things that you can see are the same as they were forty or fifty years ago – there are new materials, new electronic technology, new ideas, changes in family life and so on. In no other period could people look around them and see so much that is new. How do you, as a manager, live with this change?

- Accept change as a normal part of life rather than an irritating inconvenience. So many people find change difficult because they are not tuned in to it. If you regard the management of change as a normal part of your job, you can start to build the change factor into your business plans rather than creating highly structured plans which collapse because changes in the business have superceded them.

- Relish changes as opportunities to make progress towards your own goals rather than seeing change as a threat. An environment which is changing positively is far more stimulating than one which is stagnant. If you can see change as variety, interest and challenge, you will be able to communicate that clearly to your own staff and enable them to relish change rather than dread it.

- Learn to anticipate change rather than react to it. I have used the surfing analogy elsewhere in the book, but it holds good here again. A sea wave can be a terrific experience if you are riding with it and it can get you a long way in a short period of time. However, if you are fighting against it, all it will do is knock you over. It is certainly much easier to look for the waves of change and ride them than to insist on not moving and be pushed aside by them. The managerial King Canute cannot win in the long run – the tide will either drown him or leave him stranded.

- In order to anticipate change, the effective manager must look carefully for signs of change around him. It is very important to watch out for things happening in the commercial and social environment which may have an impact on the business, in particular on your team. We looked at this in the chapter on time management – the need to consider the environment and one's relationship to it. This means not only reading the trade press but also maintaining an interest in current affairs and changing trends in society.

- You must also make an action plan to anticipate and deal with changes. It is too easy to predict changes and yet still be taken by surprise when they arrive. Changes, once identified, have to be dealt with and managed and to do that a manager has to create a deliberate plan, setting out the likely change, how it will affect the business, clarifying goals to deal with it and when those goals will be achieved.

Preparing Staff for Change

The reaction to change differs from person to person. The young manager in his twenties may well see change as a challenge, presenting variety and stimulation. The older man who has spent years learning a trade and is content with the status quo will probably see change as a threat to an orderly existence, bringing the need to discard those skills developed over many years and the need to learn new skills. This involves leaving behind comfortable ways and moving into a new and potentially frightening environment. Other people will neither welcome nor dread change but will accept it as part of life.

Even a relatively unimportant change may be resisted by people at work. This resistance is often illogical and managers who know that the proposed change will make life better, make more profit, etc. are often very disparaging of what they see as ill-informed and irresponsible action to delay changes. The key-word here is 'ill-informed'. Information is critical in the management of change. Directors and managers have often anticipated and prepared for a particular change for years – they have adapted to it and so it no longer holds any fears for them. Their staff, however, have often not been informed and so the first announcement of the change is greeted by an ostensibly irrational response. The manager must remember that changes are greeted with scepticism initially. There is a psychological tendency to cling to old ways and to be wary of new techniques. Part of this scepticism has been caused by managers not informing staff fully in the past and so their less than eager anticipation of change can certainly be understood. Of course, many managers themselves have become sceptical about change as they have been on the receiving end of bland company statements given by equally bland company spokesmen.

How do you break this feeling of scepticism and antagonism towards change?

- Start by making sure that you manage changes in your own area. Consult your staff before you make changes that affect them. Communicate clearly and honestly what you are doing.

- If you are communicating changes sent down from above, communicate them with enthusiasm as if you believe in them, even if you do not. You are responsible for the way your team responds to change. Imagine the reaction of the Children of Israel if Moses had said 'God has asked me to convey to you these Ten Commandments. Personally, I think that some of them are a bit harsh but this is the sort of stuff that comes down from HQ these days . . .'

  If you are positive about the changes, it will help your staff to be positive. If you are negative, it will ensure that your staff will be also.

- Push your own boss hard if you feel that communications from above are poor. If he fails to tell you then you can hardly keep your own team involved.

- Make sure that your team understand the performance of the business and that you up-date them on company results and their own performance. Your staff are adults, they can cope with change if they are prepared for it. It is sudden massive changes which make people nervous. For example. if all your competitors automate their production line, don't tell your staff, 'Of course,

we will never do that.' They are grown ups and will not
believe you. Far better to take the line, 'Yes, I'm sure
that the board are investigating automation. I will keep
you up-to-date on their views.'

- Train your staff to meet the change. Changes are far less
frightening if people feel that they are able to carry out
their new role. The process of training also enables you
to explain the changes and how they will affect people.

  People resent working in a mushroom factory where
they are kept in the dark until someone comes in and
covers them with manure. Keep people informed regularly about the business, they will appreciate it and so,
in the long run, will you.

Figure 5

Managing and Communicating Change

Before communicating changes to staff, ask yourself the
following questions:

1. WHY ARE WE CHANGING?	What are the reasons for the changes? Tell them *WHY*.
2. WHAT ARE WE TRYING TO ACHIEVE?	Clarify the end product of the change and the specific measure of success.
3. WHAT ARE THE BENEFITS OF THE CHANGE?	Remember that you are selling the change – like any good salesman concentrate on how the changes will benefit them.
4. WHAT ARE THE LIKELY OBJECTIONS TO THE CHANGE?	Consider all the likely objections, and your response to them. Then deal with the objections in your communications – it will show that you are fully aware of all the implications.

5. WHAT IS THE PLAN FOR CHANGE?	Clarify the timetable for change and the involvement of your staff.
6. WHAT NEW SKILLS WILL YOUR STAFF NEED?	Explain how their job will change and how you intend to train them to learn new skills.
7. WHEN WILL YOU REVIEW PROGRESS?	Let people know that you will be giving them an opportunity to feed back to you.

Managing Changes in Your Career

Any manager who has read this book and learned to be an effective manager is certain to be promoted. Moving upwards into a new job is an exciting experience but it can also be stressful and exacting. It is important to be aware of the way to manage career changes because your performance in the first few months of a new job is often under greater scrutiny than at any other time. Typically your transition into a new role will include the following problems:

- Trying to do your new job in the way that you did your previous job. Presumably you were successful in your previous job and so you continue to behave in the way that was successful then. This is especially noticeable when managers move into new companies where the culture, or 'the way things are done around here', is different.

- The decision pendulum. In a new situation many managers find themselves swinging between extremes. Initially they do not want to appear indecisive and so they make one or two decisions which are over emphatic. These decisions back-fire, so the next decisions they make are unnecessarily cautious, if they make them at all. The problem is that of over-reaction to a new situation.

- Depression. Adapting to new circumstances is always

stressful, especially so when you have moved from a job where you have been successful to a more senior job where you are having to prove yourself again. Remember leaving primary school where you were milk monitor and captain of the football team? You went to the big school where you were a first former whom everyone bullied. You felt afraid and depressed, didn't you? Well, being an adult and a manager doesn't stop you having those feelings when you become plant manager but you should certainly understand and control them better.

The transition has to be managed if it is to be a success. Here is yet another Seven Point Plan for managing career changes.

1   Try not to raise your own expectations about your performance in the first weeks in your new job. You will be able to set yourself sensible goals when you have settled down. I always worry when I hear people say things like, 'I'm going to go in and sort out that production department now I'm the boss.' If it was so easy, someone would have already done it.

2   Clarify your new job, especially your limits of authority. If you have not been told, ask questions until it is clear in your mind. It is difficult enough to do a job without making decisions that aren't yours.

3   Discuss your role with as many people as you can. Do not rely solely on your predecessor, your boss or the personnel manager – you want to do the job in your own way without playing 'follow my leader' with your predecessor.

4   Review your management style in the light of your new job. Keep only that behaviour which is still relevant, discard those things that are not. For example, it may be useful for an engineering foreman to try to fix a broken down lathe, it is no longer useful when he is promoted to engineering manager.

5   Don't be too hard on yourself. Expect mistakes but review them carefully to make sure they are not repeated.

6   Accept that transition is stressful. Read chapter 10 once more.

7   Only experiment with new types of behaviour when you are confident. By all means, let go of your past behaviour and try to develop a new management approach to deal with problems but don't take risks until you are more settled. You have moved jobs, your new staff will have a new boss. It is a

change for them too and wildly different behaviour may disturb them; after all, you need their help to make your own transition successful.

27
Epilogue : On Becoming a More Effective Manager

If you are reading this, you must have done one of two things:

- Turned to the back of the book to find out how it ends.
- Read some or all of the book.

If you are one of the people in the first category, this is not a novel. This is not a case of 'the butler did it' or someone riding off into the sunset to live happily ever after. For one thing, a manager's job never ends – there will always be a job of work in controlling, leading, motivating, developing and coaching. It doesn't end at five-thirty either, the manager thinks and plans constantly, often waking up in the middle of the night with an idea about rescheduling number 3 autoclave or moving the canned fruit nearer to the front of the store.

For another thing, a manager will not live happily *ever* after. Of course, there is tremendous job satisfaction and challenge; there is also frustration and disappointment. The manager's job is one of mixed blessings, some of them most effectively disguised.

If you are in the second category, you have read some or part of the book. Your reaction will vary from others because different readers approach a book in a different way. Let me deal with a few of those reactions:

'If that's management, count me out'

You may be a young management trainee or someone who is thinking about moving into a managerial position. You have looked, perhaps for the first time, at the vast range of skills and responsibilities which management entails and you may feel daunted by them. Well, keep calm. Many effective managers would be daunted by such a list of management skills and yet they are performing them effectively every day!

Like Moliere's Bourgeois Gentilhomme who was delighted to find that he could speak prose, many managers do not see the things that they do every day as process skills and yet they are the difference between success and failure.

If, however, you really believe that you are not cut out to be a manager – don't give up. Give it a try. Many unlikely people have found themselves making a success of management when they were forced into a position of responsibility. You may be one of those and you would be doing yourself a dis-service to make a decision against a career in management without trying it.

'It sounds simple, but I don't think it's that easy'

In the first chapter, I said that management was simple. It is simple in the sense that it is not complex. The skills that I have included in this book have some basic principles:

- Be systematic – do things in a logical order.

- Treat people as responsible adults and they will respond in the same way.

- Always clarify the purpose of any activity before you carry it out.

And so on.

These things are simple and uncomplicated. Nevertheless they are not easy to do at the best of times. How much more difficult it would be to follow more complicated principles. Many managers and management trainers make life more complicated than they need to – this only adds to their problems. Never be afraid to simplify and never assume that because something is simple it is going to be easy.

'I enjoyed it, how on earth do I put it all into practice'

- Before an interview, presentation, meeting or negotiation, read the relevant chapter and use it to help you plan the event. Use the book as a reference; perhaps you can keep a notebook to write down any further pointers or to generate your own checklist.

- Carry out the self development activities. Use the introspection that they generate to bring forward new ideas. Translate those ideas into action plans for the future. Write the action plans down and review your progress regularly.

- Make sure that you review all your experience regularly. Learn to stand outside yourself and review your own performance. Actively seek out other people's opinions about the way you do your job.

- Don't be discouraged if you don't seem to solve all of your problems overnight. Work on the most important problems first.

'My Boss should read this'

Buy him a copy for Christmas. At least, tell him about your copy and let him buy his own. Many people complain to trainers, 'It's my boss you want to train not me'.

- Work hard to make sure that your staff are not able to say the same thing.

- Manage your boss. If he doesn't tell you why you are doing a job, ask him. If he doesn't give you feedback on your performance, ask him. He will soon get the message and start managing you better, even if it is just to shut you up.

'I don't need all this Management Theory'

Management theory is often the result of years of careful analysis of experience. Admittedly some of it is high flown and impractical but much of it is good common sense. Read management books; keep what is useful and discard what is not. People who don't listen or read the thoughts of experienced managers deny themselves the opportunity to learn from other people's mistakes.

This is nearly the end of the book. Read some of the books in the bibliography. They are a good read as well as being useful and informative. But if you don't read anything else, go out and manage. You will learn nothing without experience but you will only learn from experience if you sit down and reflect on it.

Recommended Reading

This is a list (not exhaustive) of books which I have found to be both readable and useful.

Adair, J. *Effective Leadership* (Pan)

Belbin, R. M., *Management Teams – Why They Succeed or Fail* (W. Heinemann)

Bell, C. *The Conventions of Crisis* (Oxford Paperbacks)

Biddle, D. & Evenden, R. *The Human Aspects of Management* (IPM)

Blanchard, K. & Johnson, S. *The One Minute Manager* (Fontana)

de Bono, E. *Lateral Thinking* (Pelican)

Buzan, T. *Use Your Head* (Ariel)

Coleman, V. *Stress Control* (Pan)

Drucker, P. *The Effective Executive* (Pan)

Fisher, R. & Ury, W. *Getting to Yes* (Hutchinson)

Goodworth, C.T. *How to Be a Super-Effective Manager* (Business Books Paperbacks)

Gowers, E. *The Complete Plain Words* (HMSO)

Grossman, L. *Fat Paper* (McGraw-Hill)

Howarth, C. *The Way People Work* (Oxford Paperbacks)

Hunt, J. *Managing People at Work* (Pan)

Huntford, R. *The Last Place on Earth:* (a case study in effective leadership) (Pan)

Kennedy, G., Benson, J. and McMillan, J. *Managing Negotiations* (Business Books)

Kepner, C. & Tregoe, A. *The New Rational Manager* (John Martin)

LeBoeuf, M. *Working Smart* (McGraw-Hill)

Leigh, A. *Decisions, Decisions* (IPM)

MacKenzie, A. *The Time Trap* (McGraw-Hill)

McCormack, M.H. *What They Don't Teach at Harvard Business School* (Collins)

Monbiot, R. *How to Manage Your Boss* (Corgi)

Morris, D. *The Pocket Guide to Manwatching* (Granada)

Noon, J. *Time for Success* (International Thomson Publishing)

Parkinson, C. N. *Parkinson's Law* (Penguin)

Peter, L.J. & Hull, R. *The Peter Principle* (Pan)

Player, G. *Gary Player on Fitness and Success* (Sunday Times)

Singer, E.J. *Effective Management Coaching* (IPM)

Stewart, V. & A. *Managing The Manager's Growth* (Gower)

Toffler, A. *Future Shock* (Pan)

Toffler, A. *The Third Wave* (Pan)

Townsend, R. *Up The Organisation* (Coronet)

Video Arts, *So You Think You Can Manage* (Methuen)

Index